To Diana

Go Hoosiers

Best Wishes Always

Bob Murphy

# BRANCH

The Branch McCracken Story

Bill Murphy

authorHOUSE®

*AuthorHouse™*
*1663 Liberty Drive*
*Bloomington, IN 47403*
*www.authorhouse.com*
*Phone: 1-800-839-8640*

*Published by AuthorHouse 11/11/2013*

*ISBN: 978-1-4918-3457-2 (sc)*
*ISBN: 978-1-4918-3456-5 (hc)*
*ISBN: 978-1-4918-3458-9 (e)*

*Library of Congress Control Number: 2013920244*

*Any people depicted in stock imagery provided by Thinkstock are models,
and such images are being used for illustrative purposes only.
Certain stock imagery © Thinkstock.*

*Unless otherwise notated, all images are courtesy of the Indiana University
Archives. Permission to use images has been obtained.*

*This book is printed on acid-free paper.*

"To the core, there was no doubt that Branch was an Indiana man."
Dick Enberg

"He was a man, and all that means. He was strong. His word meant something. He was honest. I think he would like to be remembered as a man that gave everything he had and when beaten, he got back up and tried again."
Dave McCracken

"Branch was more than a coach in basketball. He tried to direct his 'boys' to what he thought was to their best advantage. I don't know of a single situation where he was wrong."
Dr. Marvin Christie

# The Branch McCracken Story

"A coach is paid not in money or winning teams, but
in the men his players become."

—Branch McCracken

# Contents

# Acknowledgements

I am forever indebted to the members of Branch McCracken's many teams for their cooperation with this book. I was deeply moved by their compassion for me and my many requests and how they cared about Branch as a coach, but even more by how they cared about Branch as a person and what he had given them in their lives.

I would like to thank Brad Cook and Dina Kellams of the Indiana University Archives for sharing pictures of Branch McCracken, his teams, and players.

I would like to thank my editor Christina Koenig for her great efforts in making this book presentable and professional in all ways. I would like to thank Ryan Murphy for the cover of this book and Kate Murphy for her work as a photographer of the author.

Finally, a special thanks goes to the memory of my late grandmother Murphy who herself made history for being the first woman in the history of Indiana University to receive equal pay for doing the same job as a man, and who provided the tickets for the games and many articles of research for this book. For as long as I can remember, we would go to her house to pick up the tickets before the game, and afterward, we would go back to eat and visit. There, waiting for me in the corner, were newspapers—sometimes stacked a couple feet high—waiting for me to take home. Those papers seemed like Christmas presents all winter, and I took great care and delight in reading them over and over.

I hope that in reading this book you will learn more about the man, Branch McCracken—for whom the court at Assembly Hall is named—and his teams. May we all enjoy the Hurryin' Hoosiers and remember the joy they gave so many.

# Foreword

I met Branch McCracken in the winter season in 1948. He invited me to the campus and extended an invitation to IU that fall. I was a senior at Southport High School and was planning to attend IU as a premed student. My high school basketball coach was Jewel Young, who was an All-American from Purdue in 1937 and 1938. Those years were the first for Branch as a coach for IU. He knew Jewel very well. I was intimidated when I first met Branch. He was bigger than I had expected. I relaxed when he spread his wide smile and extended his enormous hand, which I was proud to grasp. His hair was greying. We ascended a flight of stairs to his office and I had trouble keeping up with him. He was exceptional in his appearance, behavior, and conversation. He explained that I could register for my classes next fall earlier than other students. Classes filled quickly and he wanted the basketball players in the Fieldhouse by 2:30 p.m. NCAA rules prevented basketball practice before the middle of October. We had to run the cross-country course until then. Branch would drive his car behind us, bumping the last guy with the front bumper and honking the horn. The song "Mule Train" was popular then, and Branch would be shouting the song out the window. I was never first, but I was also was never last.

I was fortunate to have played with Bill Garrett. Bill was African-American and was Indiana Mr. Basketball in 1947. Branch and IU's dean, Herman Wells, deserve to be forever thanked and remembered for recruiting the first African-American to play basketball at IU and the Big Ten. Jackie Robinson was breaking the racial barrier in the major league baseball at the same time, and there was a lot of racial tension. We tried to stay in student unions on away games, but that was not always possible. Branch and Herman Wells would always stand up for Bill when the occasion arose.

I owe a great deal to basketball and Branch McCracken for my 60-year career in family medicine. I have been very fortunate to have been one of "Mac's Boys." Smoking, booze, and drugs were becoming a real problem in kids in the '60s and '70s. Dr. Kerner, an associate, and I started a very successful challenge to this problem. I recruited a basketball team from the medical staff of St. Francis Hospital, and we challenged the athletic staff of central Indiana high schools in what was called the "DOCS vs. JOCKS vs. DRUGS" basketball game. Dr. Kerner was the manager and I was the coach. We also played the Indianapolis police department in several games at Conseco Fieldhouse. All the proceeds went to the school drug program. We raised over $150,000 in 25 years of the games. The Indianapolis Star referred to me as the only "physician specialist" in basketball. I recruited several IU alumni stars as "ringers," including John Laskowski, Wayne Radford, Chuck Franz, Brian Horning, and the Van Arsdales. My record was 21–4. The opposition brought in an occasional "ringer," as well. I was introduced as one of "Mac's Boys."

Branch gave me a wonderful recommendation to medical school when I applied. His recommendations were both verbal and by letter. I completed the 96 hours of required premedical hours in 3 years and entered medical school in the fall of 1951.

Branch was the first coach whose major offense was the fast break. The 1953 Indiana National Champions were called the Hurryin' Hoosiers. I discussed this with former teammates Lou Watson, Bill Garrett, Bill Tosheff, Frank O'Bannon, and others, and we all agree that we would always want to be known as the Hurryin' Hoosiers. Branch was more than a coach. He would help us with schoolwork, personal problems, future careers (as he did with me), and with financial difficulties. He would have us over for Christmas dinner when we had to stay on campus to practice over the holidays. The Hurryin' Hoosiers will always continue thanks to a great coach like Branch. I am very pleased to present this foreword and to be a small part of this great book dedicated to honor a Great Hoosier.

Dr. Marvin Christie
Member of the '4950 Team

*Marvin Christie*

# The Beginning

I first fell in love with Branch McCracken and Indiana Basketball before my fifth birthday. I came in at the end of the brilliant careers of Big Don Schlundt and Bobby Leonard. I grew up idolizing Archie Dees, Hallie Bryant, Walt Bellamy, Jimmy Rayl, Tom Bolyard, Tom and Dick Van Arsdale, and the seven seniors of 1965.

How could you not love the fast-breaking, heart-stopping, always entertaining "Hurryin' Hoosiers"?

When Branch came to Indiana as a player (and later a coach), the Hoosiers would play in the Old Fieldhouse on Seventh Street that would be dedicated during Branch's sophomore year in 1928. Branch would end his distinguished career in what was dubbed in 1961 the New Fieldhouse.

If Indiana played away from Bloomington, you could tune in to the radio broadcast or later turn to channel four and watch Branch and the Hoosiers go after another Big Ten Championship—minus the wonderful gym smells of popcorn and a hot dog ready for any kid's consumption.

The one constant in all those years was the Big Bear, the Sheriff, Doc, or as known to all, Branch McCracken. His six-four thundering presence was unmistakable, for Branch *was* Indiana basketball. For later generations that presence would be one Bob Knight, and for generations to come it will be the energetic Tom Crean. But this story is about the mountain of a man from Monrovia, Indiana—Branch McCracken.

This book is dedicated to those generations of fans who did not experience the McCracken era of Indiana and who may have even wondered about the naming of Assembly Hall's McCracken Court.

After talking to many former players, the direction of the book changed a little because it became obvious that to really capture Branch you also had to talk about his teams and the games they played. Branch loved Indiana so much in fact that it would move his son, Dave, to say of Branch that he loved IU and he was indeed a Hoosier. So sit back and enjoy the coach, the legend, the man—Branch McCracken.

# Chapter 1

## The Early Years

EMMETT BRANCH McCRACKEN WAS BORN TO CHARLES AND IDA McCracken on June 9, 1908, in the small rural community of Monrovia, Indiana.

Branch's grandfather, William A. McCracken, had served in Company D of the Seventieth Indiana Volunteers during the Civil War. He would return to Monrovia as the owner of a drug store for the next 23 years before moving to Martinsville as the county recorder.

Branch was one of nine children in a family of five girls and four boys. Branch's father was a road contractor back in the days when, according to Branch's younger brother Bill, a contractor "was someone who had to do it the hard way, with mules and slip scrapers." Bill would recall, "We were a big family and every one of us had to work. My sisters had to work— we all had to work. It was rough but we enjoyed it. If we had a quarter in our pocket when we went away to play a basketball game on the road we were set. A hamburger cost you a nickel. A coke cost you a nickel. If we had twenty-five cents, we were in good shape."[1]

Branch was one of the most placid kids in Morgan County until he discovered basketball. The story goes that one day a friend came by with a pig bladder and a bicycle pump. They would pump the pig bladder full of air until it was almost round and then hang a bottomless peach basket to the barn, and they had instant basketball, barnyard-style. However, Bill McCracken would recall that he and Branch played in the loft of the barn on their farm with their neighbors, the Woodens, using stuffed socks because they could not afford a basketball. Whatever the original story, the result was a love affair with Dr. James Naismith's game of basketball.

By 1919 a young, rawboned eleven-year-old Branch McCracken was a sixth-grader who landed a spot on the eighth-grade basketball team. Branch would always hold on to the small-town values of honesty and compassion, and for the next three years he would grow and play on Monrovia's eighth-grade team. The McCrackens relocated from their farm to a house in town, and Branch would eventually sleep at a family friend's home his last two years of high school to alleviate crowding at his own home.

*Branch McCracken as a freshman at Monrovia High School
(first row, first one on the left) (McCracken Family)*

After honing his basketball skills for three years at the eighth-grade level, Branch entered high school ready to establish himself as a force to be reckoned with. He made Monrovia's varsity high school team as a freshman forward in the 1922–23 season. As "Mac" entered his sophomore year in 1923–24, both he and Monrovia began to turn the heads of high school observers from not only the state of Indiana, but the tri-state area of Indiana, Ohio, and Kentucky. Monrovia would join with seventy schools from throughout Indiana, Ohio, and Kentucky to participate in the famous Tri-State Tournament held in Cincinnati, Ohio. In the first year of the tournament, Monrovia knocked off several larger schools as they pushed their way to finish second in the tourney. The Bulldogs from Monrovia would complete their season with a record of 25 wins against only 3 defeats.

The 1924–25 season began as Branch's junior year, and he fell into a role that he would eventually become familiar with: that of being his team's leading scorer and primary offensive weapon. Branch was such a force on offense that he would often outscore the opposition entirely by himself. Monrovia began the season outscoring both Gosport and Cloverdale by scores of 75 to 8 and 65 to 18, respectively (remember that, during this era in basketball, scores in the thirties and forties were considered to be a huge offensive game).

Monrovia would go back to Cincinnati again to play in the Tri-State Tournament. This time, the Bulldogs of Monrovia reeled off five straight wins to capture the tournament championship, with Branch taking home MVP and Monrovia earning the nickname "Corn Stalk Boys." Monrovia would finish the season with a record of 27 and 1. That one loss came in the sectional championship to neighboring Martinsville, 28 to 23.

The next season, Monrovia would become the first school ever to win the Tri-State Tournament twice in a row as the Bulldogs ran through five straight opponents by a combined score of 180 to 50, and Branch would once again be named the tournament's Most Valuable Player. Unfortunately, Monrovia fell to its archrival, Martinsville, in the sectional finals for the fourth straight season to finish the year 26 and 2. McCracken's old neighbor and friend, Johnny Wooden, was a sophomore on that Martinsville team, and the Monrovia head coach was Herb Curtis, the younger brother of Martinsville's famous head coach, Glen Curtis.

Monrovia would finish with 78 wins to 6 defeats in Branch's last three seasons. Thus drawing to a conclusion Branch's days in high school but foreshadowing great things to come to one Branch McCracken.

# Chapter 2

---

# THE INDIANA YEARS AS A PLAYER

## Branch: The Football Player

B RANCH'S CAREER IN HIGH SCHOOL AND THE SUCCESS THAT CAME with it would lead to Branch gaining fame and notoriety. His fame was such that Logansport High School scheduled a game with Monrovia to dedicate their new gym. Branch was sought after by many a college basketball coach and programs. One day during McCracken's senior year, Pete Straub from the IU Alumni Association came to the McCracken farm to call on Branch. Straub was directed out back to a creek, where he caught sight of the powerful six-four, 190-pound youngster wading in a storm-swollen stream using his powerful arms and agile hands to pluck out watermelons that were getting washed away by a flash flood. Straub saw that he had a bona fide country boy on his hands, and a very promising athlete. He made an appeal for Branch to go to IU.[1]

However, another school in the state had also taken interest in Branch. Butler, with football and basketball coach Pat Page, had taken special interest in this big, strapping young man from Monrovia who possessed not only power but a great set of hands, quick reflexes, and speed to match—in short, a coach's dream in almost any sport. Page asked Branch to come play not only basketball but football as well at Butler, even though Monrovia High School did not have a football team and Branch had never played the sport. Page, who was at one of Branch's basketball games during his junior year, made an offer to Branch to come to Butler right then and there. Branch simply thanked Page and told him to come back and see him next year because he was only a junior in high school. As fate would have it, by Branch's senior year, Page would be hired as the new football coach at Indiana University.

Coach Dean would talk about Indiana recruiting Branch in a 1989 documentary. "We didn't have any trouble recruiting Mac," he said, "although several other universities wanted him. But he wanted to come to Indiana, and he was a great player."

Dean would go on to talk about McCracken the Hoosier player. "Mac was as good a basketball player as they are today," he recalled. "You see, he had something that some of the big boys today don't have, and that was that he was active and had speed. He could handle himself well. If any of the opposition got a little too rough with Mac, he would get rough in return."[2] In Philadelphia in 1981 for the NCAA Championships, Dean would say that McCracken was the finest player he had ever had the privilege to coach. He would add that Branch was a "big husky fellow, about six-four, with the weight to handle himself under the basket, and he could shoot."

When Branch arrived at Indiana University, he found that Pat Page had not forgotten about him, and the invitation was extended for Branch to join the Indiana football Hoosiers. Branch did indeed go out for the football team and found that he had an aptitude for football as well as basketball. Branch would join his future college basketball coach Everett Dean in a distinction in that both men, known for their basketball prowess, would score a touchdown in college football before ever scoring their first basket on the hardwood.

In his first collegiate football game, against Kentucky State, Branch was on the receiving end of a 40-yard pass play that would set up a score for the Hosiers as they went on to a 21–0 victory over Kentucky State. However,

Branch's crowning glory in football at IU would take place in what would be dubbed "the greatest homecoming ever observed in Bloomington."[3] A Minnesota team described as gargantuan came into Bloomington as huge favorites. Minnesota scored first as anticipated; however, the Hoosiers would score to tie the game. The actions of the fourth quarter were described as follows by the 1928 *Arbutus*: "Joestling, the immortal, played in the second half, but it was late in the fourth quarter before Minnesota took the lead with another touchdown on a long end run by Almquist who kicked goal also. The tangled thread of Indiana's hopes was straightened four plays later by McCracken, who picked up Nydahl's fumble and ran 20 yards for a touchdown. Balay Cooley kicked goal. The score was again tied, 14–14, with five minutes to play. They were maddening minutes, and when the gun finally crashed it's palan [sic] to the sky, unnerved spectators fled from Memorial Stadium screaming exultation."[4]

Branch's son Dave described the accounts of that play, saying his father told him that when he picked up the fumble, he "heard a loud noise behind him" and it was Minnesota's great Bronko Nagurski. He would say that he "never ran so fast in his life."[5]

Branch's first football season playing under Page was for a team that would have more people than ever before witness the gridiron Hoosiers. The '27 team finished with a record of 3–4–1. McCracken's next two years in football would see Indiana compile records of 4 and 4 in 1928 and 2 and 6 in 1929. McCracken's overall career in Hoosier football saw Branch play on teams that won 9 games and tied 2 in a period of three years, covering 25 games with Branch making honorable mention as a sophomore and the All-Conference team as a junior playing end. This would earn him a contract offer from the Green Bay Packers worth $125 per game. Branch turned down the Packers because his heart was in basketball. Upon entering Indiana University, Branch was given two nicknames, one of which was "Doc" because he intended to become a veterinary doctor until he caught a different fever—Hoosier fever: basketball. The other nickname Branch would receive was "Big Bear." Branch would be given this moniker because of his size, six-foot-four, and his tendency to scowl on the gridiron or court.

## Branch: The Basketball Player

*McCracken in 1929*

McCracken quickly made an impression on Coach Dean and the other players and made it clear that he had a chance to become a major contributor as a sophomore. "I loved the game of basketball, and I had enough confidence in myself that I thought I could make any team in the country," Branch would remark. "When freshman practice started there were a lot of boys who came out for basketball who had quite a reputation. Some of them were all-state in high school and I didn't know just how good they were going to be, but after the first scrimmage I knew right then that if they were good enough to play at Indiana University then I could make the team too."[6]

McCracken earned a starting spot at center in his sophomore year, and his impact on the team was felt right away. McCracken, in his first collegiate game, would be the Hoosiers' second-leading scorer with eight points in a 34–25 win over Franklin at Bloomington. Just five days later, the Hoosiers hosted Wabash and Branch led the Dean men with seven baskets and two free throws for a team leading 16 points as IU ran their record to 2 and 0 with a 39 to 26 victory. McCracken would share scoring honors in a win over the Bearcats of Cincinnati with 14 points and the Hoosiers were 3 and 0.

The Hoosiers would open Big Ten play on January 7 at home against Chicago. The Hoosiers won that game 32–13, but in that game Branch would score 24 points on 11 field goals and 2 free throws. Branch would not only outscore Chicago by himself, but he would set a new Big Ten record for points in a game with 24. His record would stand for the next 10 years; ironically, his record eclipsed the old mark of 21 held by his coach, Everett Dean, set on February 12, 1921, against Ohio State.

The Hoosiers' first taste of the road for the Big Ten season came at Ann Arbor, Michigan, and resulted in their first defeat of the year, 42–41. Branch would be held to 8 points on the night; this would be the first of only two defeats for the Dean men on the year. The Hoosiers won their next two games with Branch scoring 6 and 14 points, respectively. With a record of 6 and 1, the Hoosiers ventured to West Lafayette. Branch would score only 5 points as he fouled out early in the second half. The Purdue great, Stretch Murphy, however would score only one basket, but the Boilers handed the Hoosiers their second and last defeat on the year, 28–25. On February 4, the Wildcats of Kentucky came calling to Bloomington ,and Branch, with his good friend James Strickland, sent them home defeated as Branch totaled 10 points and Strickland 19 in a 48 to 29 victory.

The Hoosiers turned their attentions back to the Big Ten, playing and defeating both Iowa and Ohio State with Branch averaging 10 points a contest in those games. On February 18, Purdue visited Bloomington and the Dean men had revenge on their mind with Strickland's 16 and Branch's 6, although he would foul out late in the game. The Hoosiers weathered a 16-point outburst by Murphy to win 40 to 37 and gain their pleasure of revenge.

The Hoosiers then hosted their last nonconference foe in Coe College, winning 35 to 14. McCracken would have his lowest point total ever in a game with just one point. Indiana turned their attention to the Big Ten for the rest of the year. Riding a five-game winning streak, the Hoosiers would travel to Columbus, Ohio, and Iowa City for their next two contests. The Dean men would prove victorious in both games, with Mac averaging 12 points a contest.

On March 3, the only other team to defeat the Hoosiers in 1928, the Michigan Wolverines, would venture to Bloomington. McCracken and Strickland would combine for 31 of Indiana's 36 points as the Hoosiers edged Michigan 36 to 34 and pushed the winning streak to eight games. The last game of the '28 season would be played in Illinois with the Hoosiers knowing that a win would guarantee a Big Ten Championship. Branch scored only 2 points and the game was tied 22 to 22 at the end of regulation. The Dean Men would outscore Illinois 5 to 1 in overtime to wrap up a share of the Big Ten Championship, closing the season on a nine-game winning streak and ending the season with a 15 and 2 mark. For Branch, personally, he would conclude his sophomore season on a Big Ten Championship team while ending up in a tie for second in the Big Ten individual scoring race, connecting on 46 field goals and 31 free throws for a total of 123 points, just 6 behind the league leader, Osterbaan of Michigan, with 129. He would score 123 of Indiana's 474 points and had Coach Dean pleased with the prospect of having his big, young center back for two more years. Because the 1927–28 Hoosier team was the winningest in school history and because, as we have learned over the many decades of sports, winning breeds interest, tickets were hard to come by in Indiana's 2,400-seat Men's Gym. The trustees authorized the building of a new 8,000-seat arena that would be opened for the '28–29 season.

After Branch's sophomore season, he was showing a glimpse of the player that would go on to become the most prolific scorer in Big Ten history to that point in time.

"We found out about Mac's ability in the pivot in one game when he was hurt and probably shouldn't have been playing," Coach Everett Dean would say. He went on to add, "But Mac wanted to play so badly, and there was no holding him. He said he'd stand around the basket and get the rebounds and he did. What he also did was take the ball in the middle and wait until one of the players could move around him, and then he would feed the ball to him. He also found out that he could fake the man behind him, then wheel around, take a couple of steps, and put the ball in the basket himself. He was the first man to play the true pivot in the Big Ten."[7]

## Mac's Junior Year

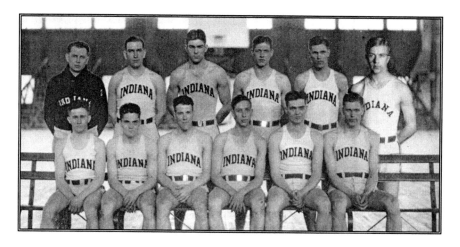

Mac's junior year at Indiana coincided with the opening of the magnificent new $300,000, 5,000-seat Fieldhouse. The 1928–29 season would be Dean's fifth at the helm of the Hoosiers after two cochampionships and two second-place finishes in his first four years.

This squad would rely on returning starters from last year's Big-Ten champs, and with that in mind, a repeat championship was anticipated.

The season opened against Washington University of St. Louis. This game was played on December 8, and Washington walked away one-point victors, 31 to 30. In this contest, Branch was the first person to score in the New Fieldhouse, hitting a free throw and totaling 5 points in the game. Indiana's second game of the season was against Pennsylvania on Thursday, December 13, at 8:15 p.m. in what would be the dedication game of Indiana's Fieldhouse. Before a sellout crowd of 8,000, Indiana raced out to a halftime lead of 19–11. Branch would lead Indiana with 9 points, and the Hoosiers would even their season record at 1 and 1 with a 34 to 26 victory over Pennsylvania.

*Program from Indiana Fieldhouse Dedication, Branch would*
*be the first person to score in this field (Murphy Collection)*

With the Hoosiers' record even at 1 and 1, they visited South Bend, and behind McCracken's 10 points, defeat the Irish 29 to 17. A visit to Pittsburgh would provide Indiana with its second loss, 51 to 31, despite McCracken's 8 points and best friend Strickland's 14. Branch would lead the Hoosiers to their third win, a 41 to 29 contest over Missouri, with 14 points. The Hoosiers then lost three of their next four games, with Branch being held below double figures except for his 11 against Purdue.

On January 21, Branch would score 11 and Strickland 12 as Indiana cruised past Minnesota, 41 to 22, to even their record at 5 and 5; however, the Hoosiers would lose their fine guard, Robert Correll, who graduated at the end of the first semester, and forward Dale Well's grades would be poor enough to remove him from the team. The loss of these two players, despite the presence of McCracken and Strickland, doomed the Hoosiers' chances for the rest of the year. Indiana lost their next five games, and Coach Dean faced his worst record at Indiana. Branch would score 12 and 20 points to lead Indiana to finishing victories over Illinois and Iowa, but the Hoosiers would end Branch's junior year with a record of 7 and 10, and finish eighth in the Big Ten.

## Branch's Senior Year

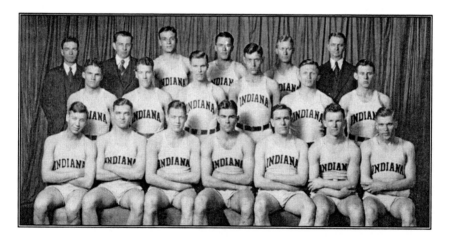

The new decade ushered in Branch's senior year. The Hoosiers would return their top two scorers in Branch and Strickland.

The season started almost as if it were a continuation of the previous year. In the opening game, DePauw beat the Hoosiers on a shot in the final minute, 26 to 24, despite the fact that McCracken would total 19 of Indiana's 24 points. Jim Strickland would be the only other Hoosier to score, with 5.

*Branch in his senior year, 1930.*

Next up, a very good Pittsburgh ball club handed the Hoosiers their second straight defeat of the season, despite McCracken's 15 points, 35 to 31. Indiana would go on to lose two more, for four straight defeats, before finally righting themselves with a 36 to 24 victory over Chicago at Chicago, behind Branch's 16 points. The Hoosiers would split the next two contests and host Wisconsin on January 23. McCracken hit a shot to tie the game at 19–19 in regulation, but Wisconsin would prevail in overtime, 23 to 21.

The Hoosiers now sat at 2 wins and 6 losses for the season. They traveled to St. Louis to take on Washington University. McCracken led the way with 13 as Indiana won, 33–21. The Hoosiers would continue their winning ways with three more wins against Big Ten foes Ohio State, Northwestern, and Chicago. In those contests, Branch averaged 15 points a game, with a high of 18 points against Northwestern.

Indiana would then lose a close one to Michigan, 21 to 18, before reeling off two more victories over Ohio State and Minnesota. McCracken would lead the way in both games with 14 and 17 points, respectively. With a record of 7 and 3 in the Big Ten, the Hosiers had only two contests to go. They fell to both Wisconsin and Minnesota on the road to finish the season with a record of 8 and 9 and a conference record of 7 and 5, good enough for fourth place.

Branch finished his playing career in 1930 as the Big Ten and Indiana all-time leading scorer. He broke Purdue's Murphy's single-season Big Ten mark with 147 points in 1930 and received both All-Conference and All-American honors during the 1929–30 season and All-Conference his junior year, as well. He would finish his three-year career with 366 points, which was more than a third of Indiana's team total scoring for those three seasons and would set the career scoring mark at IU at that time (and this was during a time when there was a center jump after every goal score—control of the tip would mean control of the ball and thus the game; and at six-foot-four, Branch got more than his share of the tips). He was also one of the first collegians to use the one-handed push shot. Branch would later say, "I was a bit self-conscious at first because I was often the only man on the floor who used the shot. But I didn't overdue it and after a while it felt natural."[8] All in all as a player for Indiana, Branch would bring glory to Old IU.

*Branch as Indiana player 1930*

# Chapter 3

## A PSYCHOLOGY OF COACHING AND TEACHING

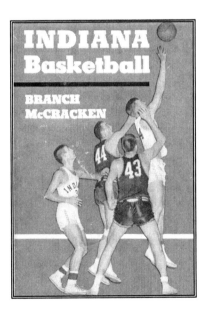

*Branch's book on basketball, published in 1955.*

"A COACH IS PAID NOT IN MONEY OR WINNING TEAMS, BUT IN THE men his players become." This is the last sentence in the first chapter of Branch McCracken's book, *Indiana Basketball*, published in

1955 by Prentice Hall. This one sentence sums up the philosophy and life of Emmett Branch McCracken.

When writing a book about someone, if you can use their own words to describe their outlook on their own work, the question begs to be asked, why wouldn't you? Using that approach, we will look to understand Branch's philosophy on coaching from his book, *Indiana Basketball*. The quotations in this chapter originate in chapter one of that book, "The Coach, His Psychology and His Players."[1]

The mere fact that Branch began his book of Indiana Basketball by stating his philosophy shows the importance he would place on this aspect of life. He began by writing about what he thought spectators or fans are all able to see while watching a basketball game. He states that they can observe "team play, excellent ball handling, a variety of shots, clever foot-work, good defense, a goal shooting accuracy." He would go on to say that there were, however, important factors that would mean the difference between a great team and an average one; that there are unseen assets that both a coach and his players must develop over the season; that this development must begin from the time "a coach and his players first meet, until the boy's playing days are over."

Branch listed these unseen assets as one "Team Spirit," which he considered to be made up of "morale and cooperation," and two, a "Driving Desire to learn, to improve, to excel, and to win." A third asset would be "Self-Discipline," which consisted of, "mental, emotional, and physical discipline." The fourth asset was "Pride in himself, teammates, school, coach, and community," and a fifth asset was, "Confidence in himself, in his own and his teammates' ability, in his coach, and in the system of play." Finally the sixth asset would be "Leadership to direct, to encourage, to take responsibility." Branch felt that if all these assets were acquired, a team of average ability could develop into an outstanding team.

Branch viewed the coach as a teacher, stating that "thorough knowledge of basketball fundamentals, drills, team offense, and team defense, does not necessarily mean that a coach will be successful. In spite of the press clippings declaring that he was a great basketball player and know how to execute all fundamentals and systems, a coach may still fail. Neither knowledge nor press clippings will develop a good team unless the coach is able to teach. He must be able to present the material so that every player clearly understands and learns quickly. The coach uses the same methods of teaching that are used in every field. Fortunately, he is able to concentrate on individual instruction when necessary."

Branch would even give his opinion of how to teach in a section he called "Advice for Teaching": "Keep your teaching simple and easily understood. Be sure the players thoroughly understand and learn each step as it is presented. Have each boy do well everything he learns. Demonstration is one of the best teaching methods. Seeing is believing. If players see how a play is run and that it will work, they learn and perfect it quickly. Teach individually for correct and thorough learning. Take the player off by himself. Work patiently and demonstrate and correct until the work is mastered. Don't over coach. It is better to do a few things well than many things poorly. Finally simplify your system and do it well rather than use a complicated system, doing everything haphazardly."

Branch would turn next to the coach as a salesman. This section becomes increasingly interesting when you compare the world of 1955 to 2013. However, many of the points made for that time and place still ring very true in today's world:

The coach is a salesman. He must sell himself to the players, to the faculty, and to the public. He must be sincere and honest in his salesmanship.

> The players must have confidence in the coach as a person. They must believe in him, his experience, and what he is teaching. Every player must be sold on what he is taught, how to do it, and convinced that by doing properly what he learns he and the team have a good chance of being successful. The coach must sell the players to each other, and teach the players how to sell themselves to one another.

The coach must have the faculty for him. He must enter into faculty functions and be willing to cooperate in every way possible. It is easy for all of us to get so wrapped up in our own field that we can't sympathize with another person, see his problems, or understand his point of view. The other person's field is just as important to him as your field is to you.

The coach must sell himself and his players to the public. Since nearly everyone in the state of Indiana has played basketball of some kind, from the barnyard to the well-coached, competitive type or is a basketball spectator, most people have an idea of how the game should be played.

Branch would say that everyone is entitled to their opinion and a good coach should remember that, so it is incumbent on a coach to sell the public on what you are trying to do in basketball and with your team. You should "sell the boys as players and individuals to the public while taking as much interest in community affairs as the fans take in your basketball. A coach should listen to criticism without losing his temper, for everyone has a right to their opinion. You should not antagonize the fans. If a coach will follow these steps then in a short time you will find the community taking pride in the team, and the team working harder to deserve the respect of the public."

Branch concluded his philosophy by summarizing the coach as a psychologist. Branch called a coach a practical psychologist, one who applies a psychology of common sense and understanding. A coach's greatest asset, according to McCracken, is his ability to remember back to his own problems when he was young, which should help him see his players' points of view. For a coach will work not only with his team as a unit, but with each individual player. A coach "can develop those assets that made for a great team if only he has a thorough understanding of and sympathy for each boy who plays for him. A coach must learn what makes each boy tick, why he does what he does, what his attitudes are, and how best to approach the player to help him. A coach must be sincere in his interest in his player not just as a ball player but as a man." Branch recognized that a player could see right through a coach who was only interested in them as a player and not as a person. He would talk about how a player's friends or family might also have a huge influence on the individual player and how a "coach's job or responsibility is to help each player improve their sense of values, judgment, and confidence."

Branch saw that the coach as a psychologist must enable each player to realize that he is a good player because his teammates made him one. McCracken would describe a successful team "as one whose players do their individual jobs well, like each other on and off the floor, respect each other's ability, cooperate, and stand together as a unit." A perfect example of this would occur in the year 2010 when Steve Redenbaugh was inducted into the Indiana High School Hall of Fame. In the program there was congratulatory ad purchased by Indiana University teammates Tom and Dick Van Arsdale, along with Jon McGlocklin, some 45 years after they had shared the court in 1965 in what was called the New Fieldhouse on the 24th and final team of Branch McCracken.

For Branch, confidence was described as a secure inner belief in one's self, and Branch would stress that his players should take "the floor confidently but with respect for his opponent. One thing we learn early at Indiana is respect all—fear none."

For Branch, it was imperative that his teams represent Indiana University in the best possible light wherever they were. This meant being well groomed and well dressed, as well as displaying exemplary conduct for all to see. An Indiana player should be one that leads in the right and leaves a favorable impression of Indiana University. As Branch would conclude, a coach was inherently paid by the men his players became.

# Chapter 4

# THE BALL STATE YEARS

I T ALL STARTED WITH AN ANNOUNCEMENT IN THE MARTINSVILLE paper on May 12, 1930: "Friends of Branch McCracken announced yesterday that the Indiana University captain and last year's center will accept a position as athletic coach at Ball Teachers College at Muncie next fall."[1] With that announcement in print, Branch McCracken was on his way north of Bloomington to Muncie, Indiana, to lead the fortunes of the Ball State basketball team. Branch was 22 years old at the time and was in fact younger than some of the players that he would coach.

One of his players on that very first team was John Brogneaux. In a 1989 interview about Branch, Brogneaux would say this about Branch: "During the depression, some players came back to school. One member of the team, Floyd Harper, was 25 years old and Mac was only 22 or 23. It was very interesting to me that Mac was able to come in and command the respect of Floyd Harper. Floyd had played a lot of semi-pro basketball. He was an excellent player. But McCracken was the leader, and he was the accepted leader, and he was the coach and everyone knew it. We all did what he asked us to do because we wanted to be successful."[2] While at Ball State, Branch busied himself in two other areas as well as coaching the Cardinals. Dave McCracken would say that his father had turned down the Green Bay Packers offer because not only did he want to coach basketball, but he wanted to play professional basketball as well. Branch did in fact briefly play professional basketball. He graduated in time to join the Osh Kosh All-Stars and led them to a 30–23 win over the Chicago Majestics and the 1930 Midwest Pro Championship. He would then play for the Fort Wayne Hoosiers of the American Basketball League. He played for the Indianapolis Kautskys, where he would team up with his old boyhood friend, Johnny Wooden, in the newly formed National Basketball League. After the NBL folded, McCracken joined the Dayton Metropolitans and a semi-pro team in Richmond, Indiana.

His third and most important adventure at Muncie, other than coaching the Redbirds and playing professional basketball, was the courtship of Mary Jo Pittenger, the president's daughter. They would marry on Sunday, December 20 at 5:30 p.m. Mary Jo would describe in Ray Marquette's book, *Indiana University Basketball*, how her dad, the university president, spoke to her about their engagement: "When Mac and I were first engaged, my father called me into his office one day and asked me point-blank what qualifications I had to be a good coach's wife. He told me that the university had a fine young basketball coach and he didn't want his career to be impaired. So we sat there for four hours and discussed how I could help Mac in his profession. I honestly believe that my father was more interested in Mac's future then he was in his daughter's ability to be a wife."[3]

In marrying Mary Jo, McCracken would have his biggest victory ever in Muncie. Mary Jo would prove to be one of McCracken's biggest assets in getting and keeping a play for his basketball team. McCracken's friend Bill Unsworth said of Mary Jo, "She helped Branch in many ways. I remember Mac's background and athletic ability didn't lead to social graces. She helped him in ways like that. When it came to recruiting, boys would come with their parents, and well, Mary Jo was a charmer and mothers and fathers would meet Mary Jo and if Branch wanted that boy, well, they felt like they could trust their son with Mary Jo and Branch."[4] Mary Jo not only helped recruit boys to Indiana and Ball State, but she would help to keep them there. The boys would come out for two or three hours for help with their studies, and Mary Jo once described the experience as being just like a mother and her kids. She would go to the various instructors and professors and find out what a particular player's problem was in that class, make note of it, and help that player through school. With Mary Jo's help, Branch's Hoosiers and Cardinals would have a very high graduation rate.

Twenty-two year old McCracken would enter his first year as a head coach at Ball State. McCracken's first team consisted of these players: Cly, Toler, Kitchel, Harper, Marvin Dick, Dorwin Dick, Brogneaux, Olsen, Renner, Edwards, Tuner, Myers, Pittenger, Hutchinson, and Burns. McCracken would replace coach Parker, who was himself a former Indiana basketball player and who had chosen not to return for the 1930–31 season.

McCracken's first game as head coach would see his Ball State Cardinals host Indiana Central, the Evangelical United Brethren School from the south side of Indianapolis. The trip north was not kind to the Greyhounds, as Mac's players, McCammon, Harper, and Dorwin Dick, would scored big, for those days, and the Cardinals beat the Greyhounds, 37 to 33. McCracken's first game as head coach was not only a successful one, but a glimpse into the future of his Hall-of-Fame career. Mac's first road game was at Wabash, and the Cavemen defeated the Cardinals 15 to 14 as Ball State had trouble shooting from the line. Mac's Cardinals would return home to face Franklin, and Floyd Harper hit a shot to tie the score at 38 and send the game into overtime. McCracken's Cardinals would outscore Franklin 3 to 2 in the extra period to capture an overtime win, 41 to 40.

Before a packed house, Ball State hosted DePauw. The Cardinals would lead only by 2 at the half, 14 to 12. However, pressing all over the court in the second half, Ball State overwhelmed DePauw, and despite Floyd Harper fouling out, they would capture their third win of the season, 37 to 23. Their next game would see the Cardinals of Muncie travel south to Indianapolis for a return engagement with Indiana Central. McCammon had a huge second half and led Mac's Men to a 45–38 victory. McCracken's Cardinals had now won three in a row.

Wabash, who had given McCracken his first and only loss to this point in his coaching career, would visit Ball State. Floyd Harper again fouled out, but Marvin Dick would replace Harper and play well as the Cardinals rolled off their fourth win in a row, 40 to 30. Indiana State came into Muncie with the idea of slowing down the game. However, Mac's Men turned a 21 to 20 halftime score into an easy 42 to 30 win. McCracken was now 6 and 1 early into his coaching career.

The Danville Purple Warriors would come into Muncie hoping to end the Cardinals' winning streak. They used tight defense and greater height to turn a 17 to 17 halftime tie into a 35 to 23 victory. The Cardinals traveled to Franklin and turned a 4-point halftime lead into a 32 to 27 win over the Baptists. Evansville would be the next game for McCracken's boys. The Cardinals were as cold as the February weather outside. Ball State connected on only 3 for 11 from the free-throw line and, as described in the Ball State yearbook of 1931, "15 out of too many attempts from the field."[5] Despite the Cardinals' poor shooting, they would prevail over Evansville, 33 to 25.

With a record of 8 and 2, McCracken's Cardinals hit the road, going first to Terre Haute and then to Central Normal. They would drop both contests, 27 to 19 and 15 to 12. Mac's last home game of the season came against N.A.G.U. The Cardinals turned a 3-point half-time lead into a 37 to 20 rout. McCracken would play his reserve players for a greater part of the last period.

The last game of McCracken's first season was a road contest in Greencastle, Indiana, against DePauw. The Cardinals lost this affair 25 to 21 largely because of shooting 7 of 15 from the free-throw line. McCracken would end his first year as head coach with a 9 to 5 record.

In 1931, McCracken entered year two of his coaching career with some holdovers from year one: Cly, McCammon, and the Dick brothers, Dorwin and Marvin. The Cardinals would open the season at home against N.A.G.U. of Indianapolis. N.A.G.U. shot what at that time was considered sensational shooting, hitting 9 out of 21 in the second period to defeat Ball

State, 33 to 30. Game two was played in Indianapolis against Indiana Central. Ball State came into the game with excellent passing and great defense to win a close game, 25 to 22. The last game before Christmas would see Mac's Cardinals go to Central Normal. Ball State would lead throughout, but Normal would prevail at the end to win, 18 to 16.

After the Christmas break, Ball State hosted Centenary College from Louisiana. Mac's Cardinals would even their record at 2 and 2 with a 32 to 18 victory. Staying at home, Ball State lost to Franklin, 31 to 27. They then traveled to Terre Haute, and Ball State lost their second in a row, 22 to 21. Western State from Kalamazoo, Michigan, would travel to Muncie, and Mac's Men would send them home losers, 35 to 31. In the game, the Cardinals' McCammon shut down the Wolverines' star player, Perrigo, to help the Cardinals prevail. Ball State would then even their record at 4 and 4 against Evansville behind the excellent play of King, Cly, and McCammon with a 26 to 19 victory. A smaller Danville team would visit Muncie, and McCracken defeated Central Normal for the first time in four games, 38 to 25.

Ball State would lose their star center, McCammon, for the next two games, and the Cardinals would lose not only McCammon, but the games as well, falling to Indiana Central and Butler by scores of 33 to 20 and 36 to 22. Indiana State traveled to Ball State, and McCammon returned to the Cardinal lineup. Despite a 10 to 1 Indiana State start, the Cardinals rallied behind McCammon's 12 points to win 32 to 23.

The Cardinals' last home game would be a victory over the Spartans of Manchester, 32 to 23. Ball State's last game of the season was played in Franklin, Indiana, and the Cardinals, behind McCammon's 10 points and Dorwin Dick's 7 points, would end the season on a winning note, 30 to 27. McCracken ended his second season as head coach with another winning record of 9 and 7. Branch would be awarded the Small College Coach of the Year honors.

Season three began with a win over N.A.G.U., 38 to 14. Although Ball State led most of game two, they would end up on the short end of the score, 32 to 20. Game three saw Ball State overcome a halftime score of 11 to 10 to outplay Danville in the second period for a 27 to

18 victory. After Christmas break, Mac's Men would lose their next two games to Centenary College and Franklin. Ball State won win three of their next four games defeating Evansville, Indiana State, and Manchester while losing to Danville. Ball State then lost four of their next five to see their record slip to 6 and 8.

The Cardinals won their last home game of the year on a last-minute field goal by Todd, 30 to 29 over Franklin. Ball State traveled to Manchester and lost their season final, 24 to 18. In that game, the Cardinals failed to score from the field in the second half. The Cardinal record would stand at 7 and 9, and McCracken would experience one of the few losing seasons in his storied coaching career.

McCracken would enter the halfway mark of his coaching career at Ball State in 1933. The Cardinals traveled to Greencastle to open the 1933–34 season. Ball State came from behind at the half, 10 to 6, to outscore DePauw 15 to 10 in the second half for a 21 to 20 opening win. McCracken would play the entire team in a 33 to 13 win over N.A.G.U. to go 2 and 0 for the season. Branch took the Cardinals to South Bend and lost to the Irish, 43 to 22. McCracken played his entire squad for a second straight game. Ball State would get back in the winning column with a victory over Hanover, 40 to 26.

Despite starting the season with a 3 and 1 record, McCracken's Cardinals were in for a rough time. Ball State began a stretch of four games in which they would not see a victory come their way. Ball State hosted Centenary of Louisiana and came up one point short, 20 to 19. The Cardinals traveled to Western State and lost by 10. Staying on the road, Ball State would lose to Indiana State, 34 to 15. The Ball State Cardinals traveled further south to Evansville and lost in the Pocket City, 24 to 23. McCracken's Cardinals came home and stopped the bleeding by defeating Franklin, 27 to 17. Ball State would go back on the road to Indianapolis and lose to Indiana Central, 29 to 24.

The Cardinals proved victorious by one over Western State, 31 to 30. Ball State would continue their winning ways as they defeated Central Normal and Manchester by scores of 27 to 25 and 33 to 28. A loss to Indiana State for the second time in the season was followed by a 23 to

14 win over Indiana Central. This game would mark Indiana Central's only loss of the season. DePauw came to Muncie and avenged an earlier loss, defeating Ball State 23 to 17. Ball State would then drop two more to Franklin and Evansville.

The McCracken Men would regroup for their last game of the season and win a 25 to 18 affair over North Manchester. McCracken's Cardinals finished his fourth season with a record of 9 and 10. A story that describes what a ferocious competitor McCracken was at Ball State involves John Lewellen who played guard for McCracken in the 1935–36 season. "When McCracken got excessively excited," Lewellen said, "he wouldn't jump up and down, yelling and screaming. He'd just grab my thigh and squeeze so hard that I'd almost scream."[6]

The 1935 season would be McCracken's fifth at Ball State. After starting his first two years with a winning record, McCracken had suffered two seasons below 500 in the last two years. Ball State would host Taylor in the first game of the season for the Cardinals. Taylor had already played three games, yet the Cardinals would prevail, 37 to 20. Ball State's second game of the season was played in Bloomington against the "Scrappin' Hoosiers." Five thousand fans greeted McCracken's team as he returned home for the first time in his coaching career to the Fieldhouse, where he had been the first player to ever score in this hallowed building. Branch would face Everett Dean, his old college coach. Indiana lead at the half, 13 to 12, thanks in part to Fechtman, the six-foot-nine center, who scored a basket then passed to Kehrt for 2, and a 12 to 9 lead changed to a 13 to 12 deficit. The second half belonged to Indiana and Fechtman, as the Hoosiers outscored Ball State 22 to 7 in the second half for a final score of 35 to 19. McCracken's first trip home would not go as he had wished. Ball State would split their next two games, winning at Earlham and losing at Franklin.

Ball State returned to action after Christmas break and won a home game, 35 to 31, over DePauw. The Cardinals would host Indiana State on Friday night and Western Michigan on Saturday night. Ball State fell to both Indiana State, 23 to 21, and Western Michigan, 37 to 24. The Cardinals would travel to Indiana Central and escape with a 29 to 28 victory. Ball State hosted Franklin in an old-fashioned barn burner as McCracken's men would escape in double overtime, 30 to 27. The Cardinals, riding a two-game winning streak, would extend it to three with a 22 to 18 win over DePauw. Indiana Central would come to Muncie and eke out a 17 to 16 win, scoring the last 8 points of the game after Ball State's Bolander was injured and had to leave the game with the Cardinals leading 16 to 9. Ball State would lose four of their last seven to end the season with a 9 and 9 record.

Year number six at Ball State would bring some confusion to McCracken and Ball State's record on the year. The Cardinals would plan an 18-game schedule; however, two additional games would be played in the Olympic Elimination Tournaments, which account for the discrepancy in a 12 win 6 loss record or a 13 win 7 loss record with the two additional games. The home court would be very kind to McCracken's Cardinals, as they would win 9 of 10 at home. However, the road was a different manner, as they won 4 of 10 away from Muncie.

McCracken built a team on speed and fast passing. Ball State would win the opening game 49 to 33 over Taylor University, but the Cardinals lost to McCracken's alma mater, Indiana, in Bloomington. The Hoosiers led at halftime, 24 to 17, and Fred Fechtman would duplicate the actions of McCracken during his years as center at Indiana by being the leading scorer of the game with 17 points in a 44 to 28 Hoosiers victory.

Ball State then went to Indianapolis and became Indiana Central's eighth victim in a row, 38 to 30. Ball State, after dropping two of their first three, would go on a six-game winning streak, defeating Miami of Ohio, Franklin, and Wabash before Christmas break by scores of 29 to 22, 38 to 37, and 28 to 20.

Returning from Christmas break, DePauw, Manchester, and Indiana Central would all fall victims to McCracken's Cardinals. Franklin ended the six-game winning streak with a 32 to 30 win over Ball State. Ball State, celebrating "Dad's Day," had a huge crowd to cheer them on in a close 34 to 32 win over Indiana State. The Cardinals lost an overtime affair to Wabash before beginning another three-game winning streak against the likes of Earlham, DePauw, and Manchester. In the final home game of the season, Western State would hand the Cardinals their only home loss of the year. A loss to Indiana State and a win over Earlham would round out the year at 12 and 6.

The Cardinals then played in the fifth district eliminations of the nationwide Olympic Tournament. Their first opponent was Wayne University of Detroit, and Mac's Men would easily defeat Wayne by a score of 33 to 16. The second-round game against Central Normal of Danville would prove to be much more difficult, as the Cards would lose, 46 to 23.

McCracken would start year seven out with very high expectations after finishing 13 and 7 the previous year. Returning nine veterans, Branch had every reason to feel very optimistic. The Cardinals would start off at home against Taylor with a decisive win, 42 to 18. McCracken would take his Cardinals by train to Madison, Wisconsin, to face the Wisconsin Badgers. The Badgers were McCracken's first Big Ten opponents as coach outside of the Indiana Hoosiers. The Cardinals had some justifiable jitters opening the game, but McCracken's Cards would come back to make a game of it before losing, 38 to 33.

Ball State would reel off four in a row over Beloit, Indiana Central, Franklin, and Wabash. Manchester defeated Ball State, 35 to 33. Ball State would then erase a 25 to 16 deficit to Franklin and hold on to win in the end, 29 to 26. Ball State won two of their next three, setting up a February first game in Muncie vs. the "Fightin' Hoosiers." Indiana would lead, 15 to 10, at the end of the first half. The game saw both teams shoot very poorly, with McCracken's Cardinals being described "as nervous as a freshman at a sorority tea."[7] Indiana would go on to beat McCracken and Ball State, 31 to 22, behind Gunning's 7 points. McCracken was now 0 and 3 against his alma mater. Ball State, however, did not stop because of the Hoosiers' win; the Cards would rebound and win five of their next seven games. McCracken's boys would finish the season with a record of 13 win against just 6 defeats in a season that would include a sweep of Indiana State for the first time in 10 years.

*Branch as Ball State coach, February 1, 1937 (Murphy Collection)*

The 1937–38 Season would be McCracken's last at Ball State, and Branch saved the best for last. Branch's Cardinals traveled to South Bend to take on the Notre Dame Fighting Irish. The Cardinals would lose this encounter by a score of 43 to 28. The Cardinals then came home to play Indiana Central and again lost by the score of 43 to 28. History was repeating itself. The day would be December 11, and it would be a red letter day in the history of Ball State. The Indiana Hoosiers would come to Muncie as Coach Everett Dean faced his former student for the fourth time. McCracken had lost the first three encounters, but this day would be different. Ball State and McCracken would play what would be called the "battle of the ages." The score at halftime would be tied at

21; however, Ball State, behind Lackey's and Rudicel's 13 points apiece, would outscore an Indiana team led by Ernie Andres 21 to 17 in the second half for a 42 to 38 win. The victory would be a first for Ball State over Indiana. The 1938 Ball State yearbook called it "a victory that will be talked about as long as Ball Brothers make fruit jars." [8]

Ball State would win three more games before losing their next two contests at Franklin, 38 to 37, and Toledo, 47 to 35. The January 7 loss to Toledo proved to be the last loss for McCracken at Ball State. Ball State, starting with a victory over Western Michigan, would win out, recording 13 wins in a row and giving McCracken his best year ever at Ball State with a record of 17 and 4. Branch would receive his second Small College Coach of the Year award for this outstanding season. With that remarkable year, McCracken would leave Ball State to return south to Bloomington to take charge of his beloved Hoosiers.

*Branch McCracken, 1938.*

# Chapter 5

## MAC'S FIRST INDIANA TEAM

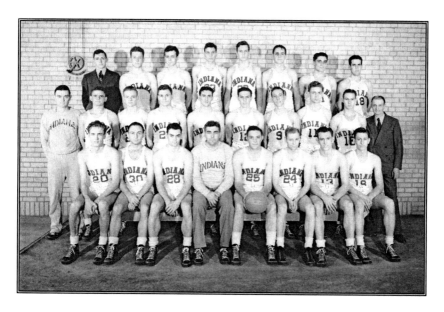

THE YEAR WAS 1938 AND THE FIRST HIGHLY SUCCESSFUL INDIANA basketball coach, Everett Dean, had, in Don McClean's words, "caught the last train for the coast." The gentleman coach from little Salem, Indiana, who as a player had brought Indiana its first winning season in the Big Ten in 1920 and coached Indiana to its first three Big Ten

Championships in basketball was leaving. The first coming in the 1925–26 Season was leaving his alma matter and going to Stanford University to coach both basketball and baseball out west. Dean's departure left an opening as head coach of men's basketball at Indiana University. Indiana was left really with only one choice—a young ex-Hoosier who had been guiding the Ball State basketball fortunes for the last 8 years, Branch McCracken. In young McCracken, Indiana would turn to its second straight former All-American player to guide its basketball fortunes.

In Everett Dean they had found a young coach who had led the Hoosiers to their first three Big Ten hoops titles; now they hoped to catch lightening in a bottle twice in succession. Dean had told Indiana Athletic Director, Zora Clevenger, that in his opinion there really was only one man ready to replace him and that was his famous player, Branch McCracken.

When Indiana approached Branch with the job, McCracken talked to both his boss and president of Ball State, who also just happened to be his father-in-law. His father-in-law asked if he thought he could handle the position, and Branch replied, "Why, it's just basketball, the same as we're playing here." His father-in-law replied, "Well then you had better accept the job."[1] With that decision, Indiana had its new coach, the country had a new brand of basketball to watch, and Indiana University would very shortly step onto the national stage with championship play never seen before.

McCracken would inherit a squad that had finished the previous season with a 500 mark but had finished eighth in the Big Ten. All-American and All Big Ten player Ernie Andres would be joined by Marv Huffman and William Johnson as returning lettermen. They were joined by a fine group of sophomores, such as Bob Dro, Bill and Bob Menke, Herm Schaefer, and Curly Armstrong. These young men would now be coached by the very man, in McCracken, that a year earlier had beaten them in Muncie by a score of 42 to 38, defeating both his former school and coach. Now young McCracken would patrol the sideline for the Hoosiers and, in an ironic twist of fate, his first game would be against his former players and school, Ball State.

*McCracken diagrams a play, December 1, 1938.*

The McCracken era of Indiana basketball began on December 5, 1938, in the Indiana Fieldhouse—the same Fieldhouse that player McCracken had christened with its first points back in 1928.

The Merry Macs, as they would be dubbed by the Bloomington press, led by three at halftime, 20 to 17. Indiana would start the second half with a defensive prowess that held visiting Ball State scoreless for the first 13 minutes as Indiana rolled to a 54 to 28 win. McCracken employed 17 players in his first game as head coach of the Hoosiers and, predictably, All American Andres led the way with 14 points.

Mary Jo McCracken would talk about that first year: "When Mac and I went to Bloomington, I told him we wanted to be known as coach and his wife. I wanted to be Mrs. McCracken to the players, and we would have our own home life. So one day, that first year, there I was in our home in Bloomington on a rainy afternoon. Dave was a baby and I was down on my hands and knees scrubbing the floor. I had dinner cooking in the oven and Dave was riding on my back pretending I was his horse, when I heard the kitchen door open and looked around. There was Mac with a couple of young men and he said, 'Mary Jo, this is Curly Armstrong and Herm Schaefer, a couple of our basketball players. Curly is having trouble with his English and I want you to help him. And what do we have to eat.' So the first thing I did was tell all three of them to go back outside and clean off their shoes because I had just scrubbed the floor. Then Herm and Mac had dinner and I helped Curly, and when we finished, the food was all gone, so I had to cook Curly a hamburger. That was the end of our own separate home life. From then on I was more or less a second mother to every player we had. I'd do the tutoring, and when they had personal problems, they'd come to me and ask me to explain things to Mac and we'd get things worked out."[2]

In year one of the McCracken era, Indiana University had received a new coach and a new academic advisor at the same time. McCracken would say later, if you can't learn from Mary Jo, you just can't learn.

Sophomore Bob Dro would recall the impression McCracken made on the players that very first year. He and Herm Schaefer were wrestling when they shouldn't have been, and McCracken grabbed both of them. "He lifted us both up by our collar, one hand on me and one hand on Herm, and just lifted us up," Dro said. "The strength of that man was amazing. We both separated and thought we had better straighten up."[3] Mac had the respect of the players and a partner to help guide the Hoosiers to new heights.

Game two of the McCracken era would also be played in the Fieldhouse as Miami of Ohio came calling. The Mac Men would be led in scoring by two sophomores in Bill Menke with 12 and Curly Armstrong with 10 in a 49 to 23 victory. Games three and four were also at home and were also victories, over Wabash and Connecticut State by scores of 47 to 23 and 71 to 38. The 71 points against Connecticut State would represent a new single-game scoring record for IU, and the Merry Macs were now four and 0. The Merry Macs then went on the road for their next four contests. The first stop was at the Butler Fieldhouse, now Hinkle Fieldhouse, where Indiana, behind Schaefer's 10 points, would won, 46 to 29. Indiana would put three men in double figures—Bill Menke, Andres, and Schaefer—in posting a 45 to 33 win over Western Reserve. Indiana defeated Michigan State for their seventh straight win, but on January 7, 1939, the Hoosiers would stumble at Ohio State, losing by 7, and McCracken would lose his first game as head coach of Indiana. Indiana would regroup and win their next 10 games to post a record of 17 and 1.

Most notable of those wins was McCracken's first win over Purdue, 39 to 36, in his first game coaching against the Boilermakers, and a payback game against the Buckeyes of Ohio State, 46 to 34, in Bloomington. Also in that streak, the Merry Macs would blow out the Wisconsin Badgers, 43 to 19. The Hoosiers went into the final two games of the season needing two wins to clinch an outright title of the Big Ten or one win to guarantee a share of the Big Ten crown. Both games were on the road, with the first contest being in West Lafayette. Purdue led at the half, 21 to 17, and never gave back the lead to capture the contest, 45 to 34.

Now it was down to Michigan in order to share the title with the Ohio State Buckeyes. Indiana would have to beat a Michigan team with a 3 and 8 Big Ten mark, but winning on the road in the Big Ten is never easy, and the Wolverines defeated Indiana, 53 to 45. Despite losing their last two games of the season, the Merry Macs finished with a 17 and 3 record and a second-place finish in the Big Ten, one game behind Ohio State.

In his first year as head coach of the Indiana Hoosiers, McCracken had repeated what his coach and predecessor had done, both finishing second in the Big Ten in their first year. The Hoosiers would lose only Ernie Andres and William Johnson to graduation, and the table would be set for a history-making year two.

*Branch McCracken, 1939.*

# Chapter 6

# THE FIRST CHAMPIONSHIP

B RANCH ENTERED YEAR TWO AS THE HEAD COACH OF INDIANA WITH great anticipation. His first Indiana team had come within an eyelash of capturing the Big Ten title, and now nearly all the members of that squad were back. All-American Ernie Andres and three-year veteran Bill Johnson were gone. However, the Hoosiers, known to many as the

Merry Macs, would return their senior leader Marv Huffman, who, though not a leading scorer, would be the heart and soul of this team. Along with their leader from New Castle, the Hoosiers would return a quintet of juniors, high-scoring Herm Schaefer, Curly Armstrong, center Bill Menke, Jay McCreary, and Berne's Bob Dro.

This team's greatest asset was its speed. Although not tall, they could follow Branch's constant instructions to run, run, run. McCracken's basketball philosophy was that players enjoyed the running game, and to get the most out of your players you had to run, run, run. As McCracken would say, "All we care about is getting the ball in the enemy basket in the shortest possible time. Our emphasis is on rolling up those points. Our defense lies primarily in our offense. Go, go, go is our watch word. Think of the ball as a red-hot potato that must be kept moving, and the faster the better."[1] These words would be repeated year after year to the Hoosier players, as Jim Schooley of the '53 NCAA champs would relate. McCracken's emphasis on the running game also led him to teach his players the one-handed jump shot—the shot McCracken theorized that, because of its much quicker release, would be much more difficult to defend. McCracken's ultimate desire was to be so quick, in such great condition, that his Hoosiers could run the opponent into the ground.

Indiana opened this special season at home on December 9 against the Little Giants of Wabash. Indiana led at the half, 12 to 9, and led by Schaefer's 8 points, rolled Wabash, 37 to 24. Two days later in Bloomington, the Merry Macs would double the score on Xavier, 58 to 24, again led by Schaefer's 14 points. The first road contest of the year would come in Lincoln, Nebraska. Indiana, behind Dro's 16, Menke's 12, Armstrong's 10, and Schaefer's 9, defeated Nebraska, 49 to 39, despite trailing at halftime, 19 to 15. Indiana returned to Bloomington to defeat Pittsburgh by 16, 51 to 35. The Merry Macs would face Tony Hinkle and his Butler Bulldogs in Indianapolis, coming away with a 7-point victory, 40 to 33.

The Hoosiers again hit the road and, in a preview of the NCAA tourney, would defeat Duquesne, 51 to 49, in Pittsburgh. The Merry Macs next conquered their second undefeated team in a row. Villanova was riding a six-game winning streak but fell to the Hoosiers, 45 to 33, behind Armstrong's 18 points. The Merry Macs would push their win streak to nine with victories over Illinois and Iowa. The fantastic ride came to an end on January 13 at Minneapolis, Minnesota, as the Merry Macs lost to the Gophers by 2, 46 to 44. Indiana would rebound against the Badgers of Wisconsin, 40 to 34, followed by crushing the Blue Demons of DePauw, 51 to 30, after leading at halftime, 34 to 11.

On February 10, the Hoosiers hosted the Boilermakers of Purdue in what would prove to be a very important game beyond its traditional rivalry. The Merry Macs defeated the Boilers, 46 to 39, behind Bill Menke's 12 points. At this point, both Indiana and Purdue led the Big Ten with 4 and 1 records. The Hoosiers would then defeat Michigan, 40 to 36, but Northwestern shattered Indiana's dream with a 4-point victory over Indiana, dropping the Hoosiers to 5 and 2, one game behind Purdue. Despite victories over Chicago and Iowa, the Hoosiers remained a game behind Purdue's club that also kept winning.

*Branch's second Indiana team defeats Purdue, 46–39, on their
way to an NCAA championship, February 10, 1940.*

Then, on February 28, the Hoosiers' shooting fell as cold as the weather outside Columbus, Ohio. While the Hoosiers would take a McCracken-like 77 shots, inexplicably, they would hit only 12, for 16 percent, and lose to the Buckeyes, 44 to 26. This would be their third loss of the season and place them two full games behind Purdue in the conference race. Indiana was western-bound from Columbus to West Lafayette with just a faint hope remaining to share the Big Ten crown. The odds appeared stacked against the Merry Macs as the host school was supported by a record-setting crowd of 9,150. West Lafayette was a place where the Hoosiers had not sniffed a victory in 17 years, and Purdue was in front in the Big Ten by two games. Undaunted and never faltering, the Hoosiers would ride a 30 to 25 halftime lead to a 51 to 45 6-point victory, behind the shooting prowess of Bob Dro's 13 points and 11 each from McCreary and Armstrong. The Merry Macs had kept alive their hope for a conference crown.

The final game of the regular season would take place March 4 in Bloomington against Ohio State. The Hoosiers had one eye on revenge against the Buckeyes and the other on a possible share of the Big Ten title. Indiana annihilated Ohio State, 52 to 31, behind the scoring of Schaefer, Armstrong, and Dro. Purdue would defeat Illinois that same evening, so Branch and his boys finished one game back in the Big Ten standings, with a record of 9 and 3 compared to Purdue's 10 and 2.

Indiana, however, had given Purdue their only two losses in Big Ten play, so when Purdue was given an invitation to the NCAA tournament, they declined since both the Purdue coach, Piggy Lambert, and the Purdue administration felt Indiana deserved to go. Although Oregon had in 1939 won the first-ever NCAA tournament, it was actually organized by the National Association of Basketball Coaches, so the '40 tournament was the first to be organized by the NCAA.

Indiana was issued an invitation upon Purdue's refusal to go, and McCracken said, "Well, we've been invited and we're going. We don't have any money for the trip and I don't know how much we'll be getting, but we're going."[2]

Indiana Athletic Director Clevenger made sure that there was indeed money for the trip, and Mary Jo McCracken went along to handle the accounts so that Branch could concentrate on coaching the boys.

The trip to the finals would end in Kansas City, but before Indiana could go to the finals, they would first have to endure a trip to Indianapolis to play the East Regional at Butler Fieldhouse. This tournament was split into two regionals: the West Regional, to be held in Kansas City, Missouri, with Southern California taking on Colorado and Kansas playing Rice; and the East Regional in Indianapolis, with Indiana playing Springfield (Mass.) and Duquesne opposing Western Kentucky.

Indiana would open tournament play at Butler Fieldhouse before a crowd of approximately 10,000 fans and numerous Indiana high school hardwood teams. Indiana trailed in the opening minutes, 5 to 4, then Herm Schaefer and his teammates began a shooting barrage that not only gave the Hoosiers a halftime lead, but would push the advantage to a 39-to-14 count before McCracken began substituting for the starters. Schaefer would lead the Merry Macs in scoring with 14, followed by Armstrong's 7, Huffman's 6, Dro's 5, Menke and McCrary's 4, and with Dorsey, Frey, and Gridley each throwing in 2 points. While Indiana was lighting up the scoreboard, the entertainment of the night might have been provided by New York referee Pat Kennedy, who kept yelling to Springfield to "go ahead and shoot-shoot."[3] Indiana would prevail by the score of 48 to 24 and advance to the championship of the East Regional against Duquesne, to be played on March 23.

The East Regional championship game would start under auspicious circumstances, as Glen Adams of Columbus would be the substitute referee after Stan Freezie of Indianapolis, who refereed the Western Kentucky versus Duquesne game, was confronted by two angry Western fans and things got a little rough.

The game itself got underway when, with only 25 seconds gone by, Captain Marv Huffman dribbled down the side, then poised and flipped in the first 2 points of the game. Herm Schaefer contributed a free throw and, after Bill Menke's tip-in basket, Schaefer hit a one-handed shot to push the Hoosier lead to 7 to 1. Bill Menke, Bob Dro, and Herm Schaefer each countered baskets for the Mac Men to advance the Hoosiers to a 17-to-5 advantage. As Widowitz for Duquesne scored, Bill Menke returned the favor and Indiana took a 25-to-13 lead into the locker rooms at halftime. Duquesne would open the second half on a 4 to 1 run to cut the Hoosier lead to 26–17. After an Armstrong free throw, forward Milkovich made a shot to cut the Hoosier lead to eight, 28–20. After the Iron Dukes cut the lead to 33–27, Marv Huffman drove the length of the court to score for the Hoosiers. Schaefer took a pass from McCreary for a one-handed jumper and Marv Huffman hit from the charity strip, and Indiana would win the East Regional, 39 to 30.

The Hoosiers would return to Bloomington late Saturday night with the beautiful three-foot trophy awarded to the winner. Each player was presented a belt buckle and belt with the inscription "Eastern Division National Champions" on it. By Monday, the Merry Macs were practicing for the championship battle with Kansas. The team would have their last local workout on Tuesday before leaving Wednesday afternoon at 5 o'clock on a train ride that would deliver the Hoosiers to Kansas City on Thursday morning.

On the train ride, McCracken would wait until the entire team could be seated in the dining area car at the same time. A funny thing happened in the dining car that day: The menus were all printed in French. The boys had never seen anything like it. McCracken solved the problem. Looking to Mary Jo, he said, "You take one table and I will take the other, and we will help with the menus." Mary Jo laughingly recalled asking Mac, "Fine, but since when did you read French?"[4]

When the Hoosiers arrived in Kansas City, they were escorted to a huge, wonderful hotel. The expectation of everyone was that Kansas, who had become a basketball program power, would win the tourney.

On the afternoon of the championship game, some of the players wanted to go to the movies and see *Gone with the Wind*. McCracken would have none of it, and he did not want his players to spend five hours in a movie house before the big game. However, Branch had to go to a coaches meeting, so Mary Jo took the boys to the show. During intermission (yes, the movie was that long), Mary Jo made the boys run around the block and stretch their legs. When they got back, McCracken was furious and insisted the team run some more.

When the Hoosiers arrived at the auditorium where the game would be played, Phog Allen and the Kansas team were being showered with gifts—much to the chagrin of the Indiana players. In fact, Curly Armstrong would turn to Schaefer and Dro saying, "Now isn't that something! Let's go out there and whip them before all their fans."[5] Of the game, one newspaper reporter described Indiana as showing more spark and drive than a Kentucky thoroughbred. On hand at the game was Branch's old coach, Everett Dean, to watch his old team play for the national title. The Bloomington Daily Telephone would run a sports section that read "Net - Crown at Stake - as IU Kansas play," but appropriately enough would run a picture of track runners right next to the article. This would prove to be prophetic, in that the Hoosiers would run the Jayhawks off the court.

The game itself started off slow with neither team able to score. Then Armstrong, Schaefer, and Dro started running, and Indiana started to take off. During the action, Armstrong gave Bob Allen, the Kansas coach's son, a fake that caused him to be out of position and take an accidental shot to the chin, knocking him to the ground. Armstrong then looked down on poor Allen and, pointing to the Kansas bench, suggested that maybe he should go over there and "sit by daddy." Thirteen minutes into the game, Indiana held a slim 17-to-14 lead, but a 15-to-5 run put the Hoosiers up 32 to 19 at the halfway mark. Indiana, under the direction of court general, Marv Huffman, kept running and would race to a 60-to-42 championship game win. After the game, USC coach, Sam Berry, said of the Hoosiers, "I knew Indiana was fast, but not that fast."[6] Huffman, along with McCreary, led the Hoosiers with 12 points, followed by Armstrong's 10, Schaefer's 9, Dro's 7, and 5 each from Bill Menke and Zimmer. Jay McCreary, Bill Menke, and Marv Huffman were named to the all-tourney team, with Huffman being named the Most Outstanding Player.

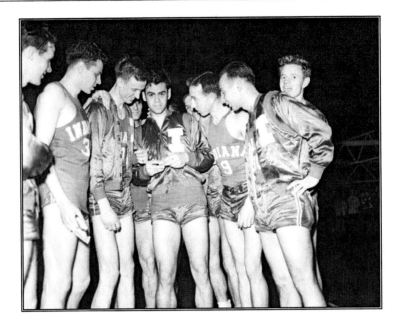

*McCracken's first National Champions, 1940*

*Kansas's "Phog" Allen congratulates Branch on Indiana's
first national championship on March 30, 1940.*

Indiana would return home Sunday afternoon to a string of cars a mile long. McCracken and the team were hoisted onto the fire truck as the parade moved down Tenth Street and out to Seventh Street and the men's gymnasium, where nearly 3,000 people and the band playing "Indiana, Our Indiana" were waiting. Each player spoke to the crowd, then Captain Marv Huffman held up the beautiful four-foot trophy.

In recapping the year, it would be a year of honors all the way around, team-wise Indiana captured its first National Championship while scoring the most points ever for a team in the Big Ten with 519 points.

Marv Huffman and Bill Menke were named All Americans, Curly Armstrong was selected All-Big Ten, and Branch McCracken was named UPI National Coach of the Year while becoming the youngest coach ever to win the NCAA Championship, which to this day he still is.

In closing the season, McCracken would meet history. After the championship game, a middle-aged man approached McCracken: "I want to shake your hand. My name's Naismith."

"Are you any relation to the fellow who invented basketball?" asked McCracken.

"He was my father," the stranger replied, "and I wish he could have been here to see this game tonight. This is the greatest basketball team I have ever seen."[7]

What a perfect ending to a perfect season.

*Branch and Howard Hoagland "Hoagy" Carmichael. Two men who made beautiful music for Indiana University in different areas.*

# Chapter 7

# THE EARLY '40S AFTER THE CHAMPIONSHIP

T WAS THE YEAR AFTER INDIANA, UNDER THE TUTELAGE OF Branch McCracken, had won their first, and the second ever, NCAA Championship. Gone from that championship team would be the captain, the heart and soul of the team, Marv Huffman. Huffman had won not only the tourney's Most Outstanding Player award, but had been selected as All-American in 1940. However, his effect on the team was more than just as an outstanding player; he was its leader. Bob Dro would say years later in an Akron Beacon Journal story of Huffman, "If you were slacking off, not playing your best, you had better watch him because he'd punch you. You did your best or you had to face him."[1] So even though the Hoosiers would return such marquee players as Bill Menke, Curly Armstrong, Herm Schaefer, and Jay McCreary, the absence of Huffman was sure to be felt.

McCracken in his first two seasons at Indiana had earned records of 17 and 3 and 20 and 3, and he had never lost a preconference game. The returning seniors aspired to make this their best season ever, and it would be a difficult task, as six of their eight preconference games would be played on the road.

The Hoosiers opened the season at home on December 7 against the Georgia Bulldogs. Playing 15 players, McCracken led the Hoosiers to a 44–31 victory. Chet Francis would lead the way with 6 points. There was plenty of support, however, as three players scored 5, including the Menke brothers, and four others would contribute 4 points each. In the second game of the season, Indiana would test the road and escape with a 3-point win over Butler. So after two games, it was Hoosiers 2, Bulldogs 0. Bill Menke's 11 points guided the way over Marshall at home, 53 to 22, and Indiana would be done with the home portion of their preconference schedule. Indiana would then "go west, young man," and face Stanford, California, UCLA, and Southern Cal.

At Stanford, Branch would face his old coach and friend, Everett Dean. A crowd of 3,000 would show up to see a classic game of teacher versus pupil. The student, McCracken, would come out on top, but not without a struggle. Stanford led, 22 to 21, at half. Indiana would take the lead at 27 to 25 and then take a 54–52 lead into the final minute of play. Stanford's Bill Cowden would go the length of the court for a layup to tie the score at 54 and send the game into overtime. Indiana prevailed in the overtime period, 60 to 59, led by Bill Menke's 16 points and Armstrong's 15. Two days later, the Hoosiers would defeat UCLA and future baseball Hall of Famer Jackie Robinson, 51 to 26. The day following the Hoosiers' blasting of UCLA, they played USC. Despite Schaefer's 11 points, Indiana would lose to the Trojans by 2, ending McCracken's 26-game winning streak against nonconference opponents.

Indiana stopped on their way back home in New Orleans to play in the fifth annual Sugar Bowl Carnival game against the Wildcats of Kentucky. It would be the first coaching matchup between two coaching legends in McCracken and the Baron of the Bluegrass, Adolph Rupp. Indiana, led by Bill Menke's 15 and Armstrong's 13, would defeat Kentucky 48 to 45. After the game, UK's Coach Rupp called McCracken "one of the greatest young coaches in the nation."[2]

Indiana opened the Big Ten portion of its season with wins over Illinois, Northwestern, and Michigan. Against Illinois, Bill Menke would drop 24 points. Star Curly Armstrong would not play in the Michigan game because of grades and would subsequently be declared ineligible for the second semester. Indiana traveled to Purdue without Armstrong and lost a heartbreaker, 40 to 36, for their second loss of the season. Curly was notably late on occasion for practice, and during one of these times when Armstrong arrived late, Branch bellowed out, "Well, I guess we can go ahead and have practice now, by God, the great Armstrong is here." Curly, always wanting to have the last word, would get back at McCracken during one practice when Branch had to take a phone call. Armstrong instructed his teammates to wait until McCracken was back to start practice again. Upon his return, McCracken was greeted by Armstrong's chant of "Well, I guess we can start practicing, the great McCracken is here."[3] So the Armstrong era was over.

Indiana followed the Purdue loss with five straight wins over Ohio State (twice), Iowa (twice), and Minnesota. In those five wins, five different players would take turns leading the Hoosiers in points. Indiana was now 15 and 2 overall, and 8 and 1 in the conference play, and one half-game behind Wisconsin, which stood at 9 and 1 in the Big Ten. Indiana would host the Badgers on February 24 with a chance at an outright lead in the Big Ten. Indiana had won 27 home games in a row, 16 of which were Big Ten contests. Indiana started the game with ice-cold shooting. The Hoosiers would fall behind by 8 at half, 20 to 12. Both teams scored 18 points in the second half, and Indiana would lose, 38 to 30. McCracken would tell the *Indianapolis Star* years later that "There's no question about my biggest heartbreak. ... That was when Bud Foster, of Wisconsin and one of my best friends, beat us in Bloomington to win the league. They went on to win the NCAA and that kept us from possibly getting two NCAA titles in a row."[4] This would be a special statement, coming after McCracken's retirement and after losses to Notre Dame in the '54 NCAAs and to Michigan in 1965, 96 to 95 in double overtime. Indiana finished the season with wins over Purdue and Chicago to finish with a 17 and 3 record. A 10 and 2 conference mark would leave the Hoosiers second in the Big Ten for a third consecutive year. McCracken, in his first three years at Indiana, had a record of 54 wins against only 9 defeats, three second place finishes in the Big Ten, and a National Championship.

Branch's third season as Indiana's head basketball coach had come to an end. However, Branch's coaching responsibiliites had not started in 1940 as coach of the defending national champions in basketball, but rather as the coach for Indiana's freshman football team. Branch would coach, arguably, Indiana's greatest freshman class of football players, including Indiana Hall of Famers Russ Deal, Howard Brown, Lou Saban, Billy Hillenbrand, and John Tavener. Branch, during his years, would coach a record 25 Indiana Hall of Fame athletes.

Indiana would approach the 1941–42 Season returning only one starter, Andy Zimmer. McCracken would tell the *Indianapolis Times*, "Perhaps only in height will our team this season compare in any way with the squad which performed so well for us for three years. We'll be young and inexperienced and lucky to finish in the first division."[5]

Indiana started the season against Wabash and came away victorious, 36 to 27, behind Andy Zimmer's 11points. Indiana would next play Great Lakes Naval Station and two former Hoosiers, Ernie Andres and Bill Menke. The Hoosiers would lose, 41 to 36, as Menke scored 11 and Andres 9 to defeat their former club. Indiana then hosted both Nebraska and UCLA and, behind Zimmer's 17 points and 13 points, would win both games by scores of 56 to 29 and 47 to 33. Indiana continued their winning ways over Pittsburg and George Washington. The George

Washington game would see Indiana fall behind at the half but rally to win, 52 to 43, with junior John Logan's 13 points leading IU.

Indiana would open Big Ten play winning only one of its first three contests. They dropped the opener to Northwestern, 50 to 40. Indiana bounced back and defeated Wisconsin at home, 38 to 34. They would lose big at Minnesota, 63 to 43. The Hoosiers next hosted Purdue and edged the Boilers, 40 to 39, behind Irv Swanson's 14 points and Ed Denton's 13. The accounts of this game are classic McCracken. Indiana has never had a coach, including Knight, who was more intense than Branch (maybe as much, but not more). *The Indianapolis Star* would tell the following story on Mac's intensity. After the 40 to 39 Indiana victory over Purdue, an Indianapolis radio station was doing a broadcast of the game: "McCracken could hardly wait until the rebroadcast started. He paced the floor, fidgeted with the dials and really gave the parlor rug a beating with his nervous jumpy strides. It didn't matter to McCracken that the game had already been won. He cocked his ear at the radio loudspeaker and followed every shot and dribble. Amid squirms and jerky explosive moments, he listened right down to the last shot and then went into a semi-collapse at the finish."[6]

Indiana was now 2 and 2 in conference play. Indiana would lose its next contest at Madison, Wisconsin, 42 to 36. The Hoosiers returned home to crush both Michigan and Chicago, 64 to 36 and 63 to 34. Behind Hamilton's 11 points, Indiana would edge Ohio State at Columbus. Zimmer and Logan would combine for 20 points in a 5-point win over Illinois. Lewis tossed in 16 and Hamilton 10 as Indiana destroyed Chicago, 52 to 20, in Bloomington.

Indiana would visit Iowa and erase a 13-point halftime Iowa lead to go up by one, 41 to 40. The Hoosiers could not hold on, however, and would lose to Iowa by 3, 55 to 52. Indiana rallied back to defeat Minnesota, 54 to 45, behind Logan's 16 points. Indiana would have just two games remaining at home. IU dug a 12-point hole at the half to be down 25 to 13, and despite 13 points from Swanson and 10 each from Logan and Denton, Indiana would lose to Northwestern, 49 to 45. Indiana would conclude the '42 season by more than doubling up on Ohio State, 48 to 23, behind Denton's 13 and Zimmer's 11. Indiana finished the year with a 15 and 6 record and a 10 and 5 mark in the Big Ten to once again finish second in the Big Ten for the fourth year in a row.

The 1942–43 Season would see a Hoosier squad return four starters minus All-American Andy Zimmer. McCracken's state of the team address would say, "Naturally we do not know how much we can depend upon our sophomores, and so with Ed Denton out indefinitely, out with pneumonia, Indiana doesn't know what to expect from its basketball team. But we do think we have a good nucleus for a team that will win some important games. We lack sufficient qualities for a championship contender; we'll let Illinois, Wisconsin, and Ohio State settle that matter."[7]

World War II had started, and so college teams dealt with wartime travel restrictions. Indiana would host DePauw of Greencastle on December 5. Hamilton and Whittenbraker led the Hoosiers to an opening season victory, 57 to 40. The second game of the season featured Wabash College of Indiana, and the Hoosiers would run off with an 18-point victory. Fort Knox would be IU's third opponent. Indiana crushed Fort Knox, 64 to 19.

Indiana traveled to Louisville to play Adolph Rupp's undefeated Kentucky Wildcats. Hamilton would score 18 with Williams adding 15.

The Hoosiers led for most of the second half before putting away a 58 to 52 victory. The win would give McCracken a 2 and 0 record against the Baron of the Bluegrass in a clash of two coaching giants.

Indiana next beat Loyola of Chicago, 51 to 43. Indiana would win in Lincoln, Nebraska, 40 to 39. The Hoosiers headed north to Indianapolis and took on Tony Hinkle's Butler Bulldogs. Indiana, behind 11 points from Williams, would win, 42 to 27. The biggest scare of the game came not from Butler, but from Ralph Hamilton's collision with the back support that led to the Hoosiers' leading scorer going to Methodist Hospital for X-rays that proved to be negative.

Ohio State would come to Bloomington to play two games on Saturday and Monday. Indiana won both games. The Monday score would read Indiana 61, Ohio State 31. Indiana continued its winning ways with victories against Chicago and Iowa. Ralph Hamilton, proving to be physically fine, would score 31 points on 13 field goals and 5 free throws to set a new single-game scoring mark for Indiana. IU's winning streak had now reached 11 games, and Indiana was not done. Staying in Iowa, the Hoosiers would again defeat the Hawkeyes, and this time, Iowa would "hold" Hamilton to just 21 points. Indiana came home to face Purdue and won by 18, 53 to 35. Indiana hosted Michigan for two games before venturing to Wisconsin for two. The Hoosiers beat the Wolverines twice and then, behind Hamilton's 16 and Williams's 17, to beat the Badgers and run their season record to 16 and 0. The Wisconsin Badgers would come back in the second game to upset Indiana, 57 to 53, and stop the Hoosier win streak.

Indiana played the final of the war-induced doubleheaders against the Gophers in Bloomington. Indiana would resume their winning ways in game one, 51 to 39. The Hoosiers would then sweep the series on Washington's Birthday, 40 to 28, behind Logan's 14 points.

Indiana would conclude the season at West Lafayette, and if Indiana could defeat the Boilers and Illinois fell to Chicago, Indiana would be the Big Ten champs by half of a game. Illinois beat Chicago and Indiana lost to Purdue by 3, 41 to 38, leaving Mac's Men with their fifth straight second-place finish. Branch would head off to war, and the Hoosiers would miss their leader for the next three years.

# Chapter 8

## BRANCH GOES TO WAR

*Branch as a navy officer.*

THE '42–43 SEASON HAD JUST FINISHED. INDIANA WOULD COMPLETE THE season with a record of 18 wins and 2 loses, which placed them in second place in the Big Ten for the fifth year in a row. Branch had never experienced a season in the Big Ten in which his teams finished lower than second place. Branch's second season in Bloomington had produced Indiana's first National Championship in basketball. But now the United States was involved in World War II. Men from all walks of life were marching down to the recruiting office to sign up to serve God and Country. Branch would be no exception. Shortly after the season had finished, Branch enlisted in the navy. This chapter consists solely of the accounts shared by his son, Dave, and his wife, Mary Jo, and will not be very long for, as Dave would say, Dad didn't want to talk about the time he spent in the war.

Dave would share in an interview given in 1989 about his dad's time in service: "Dad didn't have to go—he was too old. There was no question that he didn't have to go, but he wanted to go badly because he felt it was his duty. He went down to Chapel Hill, North Carolina, where he was in charge of the recreation program for the navy pilots. He could have stayed there for the rest of the war. He finally agitated his way out to the Philippines because he felt if everybody else was going, he should too.[1]

"I think he felt I was missing something because I didn't have a father at home at that time of growing up, so his letters were long and involved, and I have reread them. It was like he was trying to be with me, even though he wasn't. … When he came back and Mother would talk about it, it was a horrible period in his life. He watched one of his best friends go up in a plane and then crash down and was killed and that affected him. The war years were not good for him."[2]

Mary Jo would give this account: "He didn't have to go, but he felt that if his boys were going, so would he. He also didn't have to go overseas, but he believed that he could make his best contribution there. Mac went to North Carolina originally, but at that time the Air Force was having a terrible problem with their pilots freezing at their controls both in training and in combat. Because Mac had always been used to relaxing under severe pressure, he was sent to Chicago to take a refresher course. He taught that course both in the United States and abroad, and later after the war, he received many letters from flyers who said that course had saved their lives, for they were able to relax, and not tense up under the stress of combat."[3]

In coaching, McCracken had saved many a game for both Ball State and Indiana, yet more importantly during this period of time, Branch saved many a young man his life.

*Branch at war.*

*Branch McCracken and Shelbyville's Bill Garrett make history.*

# Chapter 9

## BRANCH MCCRACKEN AND THE BILL GARRETT ERA

THIS PERIOD OF TIME IN INDIANA BASKETBALL HISTORY WOULD BE a paradoxical one—Dickens himself would have called it the best of times and the worst of times. The worst of times would be in the fact that there existed a gentlemen's agreement among Big

Ten basketball coaches not to play or recruit black players. This agreement would cause McCracken much consternation in trying to observe this silent accord.

At the local YMCA in Anderson, Indiana, Branch McCracken would be the featured speaker, as he described how he was in the process of rebuilding the Indiana basketball team upon returning from the war effort. McCracken would be asked the burning question of whether or not Jumping Johnny Wilson, the acclaimed best high school player in the state, who also just happened to be black, could play at IU. The room grew deathly quiet for a moment. McCracken, trying to follow the agreement, said, "I don't think he could make my team."[1] McCracken's words would kill Wilson's dream of playing at Indiana and lose McCracken one of if not the best player in the state. It was the worst of times.

McCracken, who was in demand to speak all across the state as a featured speaker, was asked to speak at Shelbyville's award program. In an ironic twist of fate, McCracken would speak on the qualities he looked for in an Indiana basketball player, qualities such as talent, intelligence, discipline, and a good attitude. There sat a seventeen-year-old junior, Bill Garrett. Garrett was to receive the Paul Cross Award for "being a student, an athlete, and a gentleman."[2] Right there in Shelbyville, Indiana, the best of times was presenting an opportunity for Indiana, the Big Ten, and Branch McCracken.

By 1947, the integration of the Indiana University campus had become one of President Herman Wells's top priorities. One of Wells's friends was John Stewart, who was a black zoology major and had become Wells's first student assistant. Stewart would be instrumental in helping Wells see the horror of segregation and racism to the point that Wells would issue the statement, "We must renounce prejudice of color, class, and race not in England and China, but we must renounce prejudice of color, class, and race in Bloomington, Monroe County, Indiana."[3]

Within this setting, Faburn DeFrantz, the executive director of Indianapolis's Senate Avenue YMCA, along with Frank Ward, Nate Kaufman, Rufus Kuykendall, Al Spurlock, Everett Hall, and Hobson

Ziegler, would meet with Wells about the possibility of Bill Garrett coming to Indiana University and playing for Coach McCracken. In an 1989interview, Herman Wells would recall how this would take place. Wells said, "Some of my black friends from Indianapolis, black alumni, came down and said would you like to have Bill Garrett? I said of course we would like to have Bill Garrett. Well, they said, he would come if he could play. I said well, why can't he play? They said because the coaches don't play black players, and I called up Branch and I said Branch, would you like to have Bill Garrett? Well of course I would, but, he said if I did this all the other coaches would ostracize me. I said if you will take him, I will take care of the other coaches through their presidents."[4]

After McCracken's meeting with Wells, he would meet one more time with DeFrantz and his group. After some small talk, DeFrantz would say to McCracken, "Coach, we all know why we're here. You know we've been over to see President Wells. We think Bill Garrett can help your team. He's a great kid. We got President Wells behind us. Coach, we'll take care of getting Garrett to Indiana. If he's here on campus, and makes the grades, and he shows he can take the training and the discipline, and gets along with the other players, would he make the team." McCracken would add, "And if he shows he can play well enough." At this point, DeFrantz grabbed McCracken's hand and said, "God bless you, Branch McCracken. You are doing the right thing. That's wonderful! They're gonna remember you for this, Coach."[5] With this, the Bill Garrett Era under Branch McCracken would become part of Indiana basketball history.

Sportscaster Hilliard Gates would weigh in on Bill Garrett coming to IU. Gates would say of the Garrett/McCracken match, "I was delighted he went to Indiana because I thought he was the kind of basketball player that Branch could utilize to his fullest, that he would be understood by Branch McCracken. It was a great moment for both of them when he decided to go to Indiana University."[6] George Taliaferro would say, "Bill Garrett looked forward to playing basketball at Indiana University under Branch McCracken, who he had a tremendous amount of respect for."[7]

The '48–49 season would open on December 4 against DePauw before a packed house in the Old Fieldhouse. Junior Lou Watson led the Hoosiers with 19 points on 7 buckets and 5 free throws. Sophomore Bill Tosheff from Gary, Indiana, had 10, while the much-anticipated debut of Bill Garrett would see the sophomore from Shelbyville score 8 points and dominate the boards. Indiana would go on to record five more victories in a row over the likes of Michigan State, Xavier, Drake, Kansas State, and Washington. In those games, the Hoosiers were led in scoring by Watson, with 74 points for a 14.0 average, followed by Indiana's two sophomores, Bill Garrett and Bill Tosheff, scoring 52 and 48 points for 10.4 and 9.6 averages, respectively.

It was the final game in that six-victory stretch when McCracken would show his concern for his players and the team would show their togetherness as a unit. Mary Jo McCracken would recall, "I remember when we were going to St. Louis to play, and the usual procedure was for the black players to stay at one hotel while the white players would stay at another. Mac talked to the manager of the establishment, and when he was informed that Garrett would not be allowed to stay there, Branch said, 'Sorry, we'll have to move to another hotel.' That was when the man changed his mind. In St. Louis, we also found out that the team, the entire party, was expected to eat all its meals in a private dining room and none of us liked that, so Tosheff and the rest of the squad went walking around, stopping at restaurants, inquiring if they could all eat together in public with Garrett, their friend and teammate, until they finally found a place where the owner allowed the entire club to dine together."[8] While Indiana would win their sixth straight, 51 to 44, over Washington University of St. Louis, the bigger victory was one for civil rights and integration of Indiana Basketball.

Indiana lost their first game of the season to Butler in the second annual Hoosier Classic at Butler, now Hinkle Fieldhouse, 64–55. The Hoosiers would recover the next night in the Classic and defeat Notre Dame, 50 to 47, behind 11 points from both Garrett and Tom Schwartz. Indiana lost the Big Ten opener to Illinois, 44 to 42, in double overtime on a 20-foot hook shot by Illinois center Fred Green. The Hoosiers would bounce back and defeat Iowa, 50 to 39, behind Tosheff's 12 points. Indiana then went into a five-losses-in-six-games tailspin in the next few months, the only win being a 56-to-42 win over Purdue led by Tosheff's 18 points.

On Valentine's Day in 1949, Indiana would get some much needed love with a 56-to-41 win over Northwestern in Bloomington behind Buck's 12 and Garrett's 11 points. This win would be the first of four in a row over Northwestern, Purdue, Ohio State, and Iowa as juniors Jerry Stuteville and Lou Watson would have big-scoring games. They would be backed by sophomores Phil Buck, Bill Garrett, and Bill Tosheff, who provided much-needed balanced scoring to support the Hoosier cause. The Hoosiers closed out the season at Champaign, Illinois, losing to the Illini, 91 to 68, to finish in a fourth-place tie with Ohio State in the Big Ten and record a 14 and 8 season record, which would give Mac his most victories in the 3 seasons since returning from the war.

The '49–50 season, Garrett's junior year and Watson's senior year, was looked on with great optimism. Mary Jo McCracken would say of this team, "The players and coaches all liked each other very much and that Branch really wanted this team to be able to go to the

NCAA, but he realized that would be difficult without a real tall center. However, it was really one of his favorite teams."[9] Indiana's roster included Watson, Stuteville, Garrett, Tosheff, and Buck, plus a young sophomore from Corydon, Indiana—Frank O'Bannon, who would be destined for fame not as a basketball player, but as a future governor of Indiana. McCracken would say of this team, "We will have to depend upon our speed and versatility to balance the superior height we are certain to meet."[10]

The season began on December 5 in Bloomington with a 64–33 win over the Little Giants of Wabash with Stuteville and Garrett leading the way with 12 and 11 points, respectively. Mac's Men would reel off 10 straight victories, which by January 5 would have them rated fifth in the nation. The Hoosiers beat the likes of Michigan State, DePaul, Arkansas, and traveled to Carvallis and beat Oregon State twice in a doubleheader. They would win the third annual Hoosier Classic in Indianapolis with wins over Notre dame and then Butler. The win over Butler, behind Garrett's 21 points, was particularly pleasing to McCracken, who had a very competitive relationship with Butler's Tony Hinkle. In this ten-game winning streak, Garrett would have two games with 20 or more points and Stuteville would have a 24-point game. The victory string would come to an end on January 9 at Ann Arbor, Michigan, despite Watson's 26 points, as the Hoosiers succumbed to the Wolverines, 69–67.

The Hoosiers would next travel to Iowa City and lose a heartbreaker, 65 to 64. Mac's Men would lose their next two by a mere 3 points. Indiana would win their next three games, including two over instate rivals Butler and Purdue, led by Garrett and Stuteville. Ohio State traveled to Bloomington and handed the Hoosiers their third defeat of the year by a score of 56 to 55.

Indiana would regroup behind Watson's 20 to beat Minnesota. The Indiana win over Minnesota was followed by wins over Illinois and Purdue. The Indiana win over Illinois by a score of 83 to72 would be led by Garrett's 20. Ohio State and Iowa handed the Hoosiers their final two defeats of the year. Bill Garrett's 23 and Stuteville's 20 would lead the way as Indiana closed out the season with a win over Illinois, giving the Hoosiers a tie for third in the Big Ten and an overall record of 17 wins and 5 defeats. The five Indiana losses would come by a combined total of 20 points.

*Branch and Lou Watson during the Illinois game in 1950. Fifteen years later, Branch will pass the torch of coaching Indiana basketball to Lou.*

Garrett's senior season would come with more than a few questions to be asked and answered. McCracken lamented Watson's departure due to graduation by calling Watson a coach on the floor. Watson would return in the 58–59 season as an assistant to McCracken on the bench.

The 1950-51 season saw three guards, Sam Miranda, Gene Ring, and Bob Masters, handle the backcourt duties. Six-foot Bill Tosheff was at one forward spot, and six-foot-three Bill Garrett handled the middle. McCracken would say, "The main thing is that we lack size this year. We just aren't big enough."[11] McCracken would go on to say, however, that he felt the Hoosiers could still be a force in the Big Ten.

The season started at home with a win over the DePauw Tigers by 14, 59 to 45. McCracken deployed 17 players in the game, one of them being Jim Schooley, a player who bridged this team to the '53 NCAA Championship team. The Hoosiers would next overwhelm Oregon State behind 18 from Ring and 13 from Garrett. Ring would ring up 23 points in game three as the Hoosiers conquered the Texas Christian Horned Frogs, 87 to 68. The Hoosiers would travel to Kansas City to face the Kansas State Wildcats, and despite Garrett suffering foul trouble, Indiana would win, 58 to 52, with Garrett still pouring in 15 points.

The fourth annual Hoosier Classic would see defending champion Indiana capture their second championship in a row by defeating both Butler and Notre Dame by scores of 61 to 46, and 64 to 56. The Hoosiers were led in scoring in both games by Garrett's 17 points. Indiana had not only captured its second straight Hoosiers Classic title, but McCracken had defeated Hinkle three times in a row.

Indiana had now won six games in a row to open the season. However, the Hoosiers would fall at Peoria Illinois to Bradley by a score of 64 to 62 on a Braves field goal with only 14 seconds remaining. Indiana would regroup and win their last game before their conference opener by beating Drake, 59 to 49.

Indiana opened the Big Ten season on the road at Ohio State. The Hoosiers jumped out to an early lead and, behind Garrett's 23, defeated the Buckeyes, 77 to 62. Garrett in the game was as hot as you would want a player to be, hitting the basket 9 out of 14 times while hitting all 5 of his free throws. Indiana would go to Michigan State and host Illinois for two more wins before traveling to West Lafayette to try to make the Boilermakers their fourth straight Big Ten victims. The Hoosiers would place five players in double figures as their interstate rivals would drop their fifth in a row to the Mac Men.

Indiana would defeat both Ohio State and Minnesota at home before traveling to Minneapolis and losing their first Big Ten game by a score of 61 to 54. Bill Tosheff's 19 points would fuel a 63-to-54 victory over Iowa, and Bill Garrett's 22 would lead Indiana over the Wildcats of Northwestern.

Indiana traveled to Illinois with the Big Ten Championship hanging in the balance. The Hoosiers would lead by 5 with less than 10 minutes remaining. However, a fifth foul was whistled on Garrett with 6:10 remaining in the game, and without their All-American center, the Hoosiers would fall by 6, 71 to 65. Indiana closed out the season with four straight wins over Purdue, Iowa, Michigan, and Wisconsin. Illinois would edge out the Hoosiers for the Big Ten title with a record that stood at 13 and 1 compared to Indiana's 12 and 2. Indiana under McCracken would finish in second place for the seventh time in ten seasons. The Hoosiers would finish the year ranked seventh in the nation, and Bill Garrett would graduate as Indiana's all-time leading scorer with 792 points, breaking the mark held by Garrett's teammate from the year before, Lou Watson, who had posted a scoring total of 757 points. Garrett, as Watson had the previous year, would be named an All-American and first team all-Big Ten. McCracken would say of this team, "They played their hearts out and worked their tails off." And of Garrett, McCracken would say, "He's an All-American if I've ever seen one."[12]

The season was over and Shelbyville hosted an "All-American Bill Garrett Night." The weather would not cooperate that night, and a typical Indiana blizzard appeared and closed many roads. The road to integration—a long road—had been traveled by McCracken, Garrett, Indiana, and the Big Ten. McCracken would make the 60-mile journey to be there that night for his player Bill Garrett, and when the scheduled speaker couldn't make it, McCracken was pressed into action.

McCracken would recall Nate Kaufman's words that they were not sending Garrett to IU to sit the bench, as well as his own words and philosophy that he never promised any boy that he could play—he would have to earn that right. McCracken would give his greatest praise of all in front of the crowd that night when he said that Bill Garrett was "a perfect example of a sportsman and a gentleman."[13] It was indeed the best of times.

# Chapter 10

# MCCRACKEN GOES WEST?

I
T WAS 1948. MCCRACKEN HAD JUST DELIVERED TO INDIANA ITS
sixth second-place finish in the Big Ten in his nine seasons as head
coach, along with a national title in 1940. He was nationally and
internationally recognized as one of the premier coaches in the world.
Branch had held clinics not only in the United States, but in Europe
and Asia, as well. He was in demand everywhere, and many universities
desired his services.

In 1948 UCLA would come calling to Bloomington, Indiana,
offering Branch the head coaching job at the California school. Dave
McCracken recalled what would take place: "My grandfather came in
and said, 'Dave, let's go talk,' and he sat me down and he started to tell
me how great it would be in California and how I would like it and
there would be no snow. What a great opportunity it would be for me,
and I thought he was crazy. I said 'I don't want to go anywhere.' But he
talked and he talked and he talked until he finally talked me into it, and
he said, 'Your dad has been offered the head coaching job at UCLA and
he is going to take it. I want to make sure you like it,' and I said, 'Yeah,
it sounds really good, and I am ready to go.'

"Then I understand Dad went to talk to Herman Wells, and Herman in effect said, 'You have a long-term contract here and we will meet what they are offering you. We don't want to let you go.' So Dad called them and said he was going to remain at IU, and I really think that was one of the greatest things that ever happened to him.

"Because he loved IU and he was a Hoosier."[1]

Branch would remain a Hoosier with another national championship still to come. UCLA asked Branch if he could recommend someone for the job, and McCracken suggested to the Bruins his boyhood friend and former neighbor, Johnny Wooden. The Hoosiers' Hall-of-Fame coach would remain a Hoosier, and Indiana fans would forever be grateful.

# Chapter 11

## THE MCCRACKEN ERA USHERS IN COLLEGE BASKETBALL ON TELEVISION

I F THE BIBLE IS THE GREATEST STORY EVER TOLD, THEN FOR INDIANA basketball fans (for which Indiana basketball is regarded by many as at least a secondary religion), this chapter may be the greatest story few have ever heard.

Before telling this story, I owe this chapter to Paul Lennon as told not only by Paul but also through his son, Brad Lennon, in the summer of 2013.

It was the season that followed the Garrett era, a season after McCracken had produced his seventh second-place Big Ten finish in his ten years as head coach of Indiana University, a season that would usher in the Leonard, Schlundt, Farley, Scott, and Kraak era. Schlundt was a six-foot-nine-inch, highly touted freshman who would be eligible to join the four sophomores because of a waiver that allowed freshmen to compete at a varsity level as a result of the Korean War.

It would be a season that would mark the fiftieth year of Indiana basketball going all the way back to February 8, 1901, when Indiana played its first game against Butler, a 20 to 17 loss.

It would be a season in which Indiana would win their third consecutive Hoosier Classic title with wins over Notre Dame and Butler, a season in which the Mac Men would finish fourth in the Big Ten with a record of 9 and 5, a season in which the Hoosiers would achieve a record of 16 wins and 6 losses overall.

But putting all that aside, it would be a season in which IU, McCracken, WTTV, Paul Lennon, Bob Petranoff, Bob Cook, Gary Ruben, Herman Wells, and Chesty Foods would make college basketball history. It would be the world's first televised broadcast of a regular-season collegiate basketball game, and this is the story of how it all came about.

This was the brainchild of Paul Lennon, Bob Cook, and Bob Petranoff. The first order of business was to ask Carl Onken, the station's chief engineer, to see if it was even possible to microwave-relay a signal from the IU Fieldhouse on Seventh Street to the transmitter. When that answer was a yes, then the next course of action was to seek permission from President Herman Wells and Athletic Director "Pooch" Harrell. The response took both Lennon and Petranoff by surprise. Both Wells and Harrell were concerned about fans not showing up to the game if it was televised. Harrell's exact response was, "Why would anyone pay a dollar for a ticket to our game if they can see it free on TV?" Obviously, circumstances have changed over the years, from free TV to the Big Ten Network and paid television.

Lennon didn't blink. His response was, "How about if we buy the empty seats at a dollar apiece." He would pull a number out of the air, of say 750 people staying home and not coming to the games. He proposed that they "would pay Indiana 750 dollars in advance, and if that's not enough, we can adjust it for the next game." With that very meeting, television rights fees would begin. Both Harrell and Wells, while expressing doubts that they could get anyone to pay that kind of money, agreed to allow WTTV to broadcast the games.

The first two steps were done, but before Lennon could get too excited, Bob Petranoff said to him, "Paul, don't get too excited. Who's going to pay IU? And who's going to pay WTTV for the airtime?

And who's going to pay you?" Of course Lennon, the 24-year-old sportscaster, hadn't a clue. But Lennon had a vision, and he really wanted this to happen—to put IU basketball on TV and to be the one to broadcast the games. Motivation can be a powerful incentive, so Lennon drove to Indianapolis to meet with Gary Ruben, who had a new client in Terre Haute, Chesty Foods. With Eckrich meats already sponsoring the television of the high school tournament, then maybe Chesty Foods and Chesty Potato Chips would be a perfect match; after all, people would sit down with a bowl of chips and watch the game. Ruben asked how much it would cost Chesty per game. Lennon would reply totally off the cuff, "2,500 dollars a game." Ruben's next question was, "How many commercials would they get?" Lennon would again answer of the cuff, saying, "about 12, depending on timeouts." Ruben could not give Lennon an answer that day but promised that he would let him know soon.

Two days later, he would call Lennon to say that they would take all 11 games. With that phone call, Chesty Potato Chips would become IU basketball's first television sponsor.

The first game was played on December 6, 1951, against Valparaiso at the Old Fieldhouse on Seventh Street. The game was a sellout, but IU would keep the $750 fee. The Old Fieldhouse was a field of dirt covered by a roof, surrounded by limestone walls, of course. A portable basketball court would sit in the middle. It was a dim, dark place by TV standards, so lights had to be added. They were hung quickly from steel beams. WTTV had two black-and-white cameras that were taken from the Bloomington studios right after the news, brought to the Fieldhouse, and then taken down right after the game and rushed back to the studios for the 11 o'clock news.

The press box was a wooden deck above the south stand of bleachers. Bob Cook, who was an assistant athletic director and publicity man for the university, would do the statistics for the game while Lennon would do the play-by-play, all the commercials (which would be live, as was the halftime), and the postgame summary. Lennon and Cook would sit above the noisy student body for the nearly three-hour broadcast. Petranoff was located in a cold remote truck calling the shots. While in the booth, Gary Ruben would hand Lennon a bag of Chesty Potato Chips at the opening and each timeout for the commercials, all of which were ad-libbed on the spot.

Paul Lennon would say, "That first night, I was like a deer staring into the headlights. When the red camera light came on and Gary Ruben handed me that bag of Chesty Potato Chips, I just suddenly blurted, 'I've got my ticket, have you got yours? This 39-cent size of Chesty Potato Chips is your ticket to tonight's game and all the other games coming up.'"

*Paul Lennon broadcasting the first ever televised regular season college basketball game. He has his ticket, do you have yours? (Courtesy Brad Lennon)*

With that phrase, the Chesty Foods business exploded. Before that game, they were just another chip; after the games, all over central Indiana, store shelves were empty of Chesty Chips. Overnight, Chesty took a dominant position in the market for potato chips. Paul would relate how many of their competitors simply stopped trying and some would even close their doors. Chesty Foods, which at the time operated with one shift, would quickly add shifts two and three. This was the power of television advertising and the draw of Branch McCracken and Indiana Basketball.

As for the game itself, Indiana defeated Valparaiso, 68 to 59. The Hoosiers would trail at half by 2, 27 to 25, but they would build up a lead of 13 midway through the second half. The Mac Men, as they were called, were led in scoring by sophomore forward Dick Farley with 19 points. Miranda and Leonard would each account for 4 field goals and 1 free throw for 9 points apiece. Masters would have 10 and Kraak 8. Freshman Schlundt in his first collegiate game would produce only 6 points on 1 of 5 shooting from the field, while hitting on four free throws. All in all, 13 Hoosiers would play in that first televised game. Branch's team would leave the court the same way they had entered it, by trotting over a path of plywood laid from the court to the dressing room to keep their shoes clean. Except for the December 22 game against Kansas State, with the students gone for Christmas Break, Mac's Hoosiers would play before a packed house every night, and Indiana would keep the $750 every game.

It was a season with a glimpse into the future—the nine sophomores and one freshman and the notoriety and success they would bring to Indiana University. By the '52–53 season, Indiana would want $2,500 per game, and they would get it.

The season was right there for everyone to see as long as you had your ticket. Got your chips? I've got mine. Let's watch.

*Plaque to first broadcast in old fieldhouse (Courtesy Brad Lennon)*

# Chapter 12

# THE '53 CHAMPIONS: A TEAM FOR THE AGES

THE '52 SEASON ENDED WITH INDIANA FINISHING FOURTH PLACE IN the Big Ten with a 9 and 5 record. They would again be champions of the Hoosiers Classic and would complete the season with an overall record of 16 and 6. The Hoosiers had introduced to the Big Ten and college basketball a truly great freshman in big Don Schlundt of whom McCracken would say, "I've got this great basketball prospect who is also a fine scholar." One professor would ask Branch how he knew he was such a fine scholar. Branch's reply was, "Well, he's six-nine isn't he?"[1]

So the calendar had turned over to the '52–53 season, and what a wonderful year it would prove to be for both Branch and Indiana. Indiana would start the season with the loss of three of its outstanding guards. Sam Miranda and Bob Masters had graduated, while five foot-nine sparkplug Sam Esposito had left school to pursue his dream of playing Major League Baseball, which he would play for the next 10 years.

However, for both Branch and the Hoosiers, the cupboard was far from bare. In fact, juniors Bob Leonard, team captain Charlie Kraak, Dick Farley, jack Wright, Ron Taylor, Lou Scott, and Jim Deakyne would join a sophomore group headed by Don Schlundt, Phil Byers, Dick White, Burke Scott, Paul Poff, Don Henry, James Field, William Ditius, and Goethe Chambers. The lone senior on the team would be scholar and leader Jim Schooley, who would watch over the group.

The first move McCracken made would prove to be most instrumental in this champion season. McCracken moved Leonard, who had split time between guard and forward, to being a full time guard. Schlundt, who had averaged 17.1 points his freshman year, and Leonard, who had averaged 14.5 the year before, would jump their averages to 25.4 for Schlundt and 16.3 for Leonard, earning for themselves the nicknames of Mr. Inside and Mr. Outside, respectively.

Charlie Kraak, who was a monster on the glass, was considered by many the best rebounder in the Big Ten. Burke Scott and Dick Farley rounded out the starting five. Scott was a great ball handler who could set up Schlundt, Farley, and Kraak in the post for key baskets all season long. In the summer of 2013, Jim Schooley would say of Burke Scott, "That was Scott's game to catch the guy dribbling down the court from behind and just take over the dribble. He would steal the ball a lot that way. He was very quick and very fast."

Schooley would recall McCracken's warning to the team to "be sure you win at home because on the road it is very difficult." For this season, however, McCracken's Hoosiers could do little wrong and they would win eight out of nine on the road in the Big Ten. However, McCracken would prove to be prophetic as the Hoosiers' only three losses of the season would come on the road away from Bloomington.

Indiana would open the season on December 1 at home against Valparaiso before 8,300 screaming fans. The Hoosiers were led by their backcourt tandem of Scott and Leonard with each scoring 16 points to defeat the Crusaders, 95 to 56. Charlie Kraak would add 13 points and 12 boards to the cause. Next, Indiana traveled to South Bend to take on the Fighting Irish. Notre Dame was ranked thirteenth, while in the coaches' poll Indiana was ranked eighth.Indiana would trail 28 to 41 at half but would mount a second-half comeback that enabled the Hoosiers to lead 70 to 69 with just 12 seconds remaining. With Hoosier reserve Jim Deakyne at the line shooting two free throws, the Hoosiers looked to have the game in hand. Deakyne, however, missed both free throws and Notre Dame guard Jack Stephens took the rebound the length of the court for a layup with 2 seconds showing on the clock, and the Hoosier's hopes were crushed—a 71 to 70 defeat. Indiana would next visit Kansas City to take on second-ranked Kansas State Wildcats. The Hoosiers would have the entire starting lineup score in double figures, led by Dick Farley's 18, while Leonard and Schlundt each would throw in 16 points, but the Wildcats would score twice in the last 35 seconds to give the Hoosiers their second loss in a row, 82 to 80.

The Big Ten had decided to try a complete round robin schedule so each school would play one another twice—once at home and once on the road. As a result, the Hoosiers would move into the Big Ten part of the schedule after only three games. The Hoosiers' lone remaining out-of-conference game would come on the second of February against Butler at Bloomington. Schlundt would score 33 points, supported by Scott's 15, White's 13, and Byers' 11, as Indiana whipped their neighbors to the north, 105 to 70.

Indiana would open Big ten play returning home to Bloomington against Michigan. The Hoosiers defeated the Wolverines by 28, 88 to 60. Schlundt would lead all scorers with 24. The halftime score would be an unbelievable 66 to 36.

Indiana's first road test would come at Iowa City as Mr. Inside and Mr. Outside would lead the Hoosiers in scoring with 27 and 24 points, respectively. Next up would be a repeat contest with Michigan. This time the Wolverines led at halftime by 1, 49 to 48. Indiana would have a dog fight on their hands but would prevail, 91 to 88, behind Schlundt's 33 points. The Michigan road trip culminated with a 69-to-62 victory over the Spartans of Michigan State. For the second game in a row, Schlundt would go for over 30 points, and Indiana was now 4 and 0 in the Big Ten. Number19, Minnesota, invaded Bloomington on January 10, and the Hoosiers would escape with a 3-point win, 66 to 63, behind Schlundt's 17, Farley's 16, and Leonard's 15.

*Branch gives instructions to Don Schlundt as Bobby Leonard and Dick Farley, drinking, look on, January 10, 1953.*

Indiana would then travel to Columbus to take on the Buckeyes. Leonard led the way with 10 field goals and 2 free throws for 22 points, and Indiana left with a 20-point win, 88 to 68.

It was January 17, and Bloomington was the stage for the game of the year between number 4 Illinois and number 6-rated Indiana. Indiana would emerge victorious in two overtimes, 74 to 70. Schlundt would score 22 points and haul in 11 rebounds but would foul out in the first overtime, while Illinois star center, Johnny Red Kerr, would be held to 6 of 30 shooting for a total of 15 points. Leonard would add 18, Farley 16, and White 10 to help in the cause. The Hoosiers next traveled to Purdue, and Mr. Inside and Mr. Outside again would lead Indiana in scoring, combining for 47 points, and the Mac Men would leave 88-to-75 victors.

The Hoosiers hosted and defeated Wisconsin, 66 to 48, then defeated the Spartans, 65 to 50, behind Schlundt's 30-point explosion. Indiana would travel to Wisconsin and escape with a 2-point win, 72 to 70. Again, Schlundt would pace four scorers in double figures with 25.

Indiana would win their fourteenth game in a row with a 14-point victory over Ohio State. The Boilermakers would visit IU for a thorough drubbing, 13 to 78 setting a Big Ten record. Indiana would have six players in double figures, led by Schlundt's 31, with 16 by Leonard, 15 by Farley, 13 each for Scott and Poff, and 10 by Kraak.

There were now only four games remaining in the Big Ten season, the next being a return engagement with Illinois. A win for the Hoosiers would all but wrap up McCracken's first Big Ten Championship. Indiana jumped out to a 7-point lead and took a 43-to-37, 6-point lead into the locker room at the half. Indiana would begin the second half by running off on an 8 to 0 run and would push the lead to 51 to 37. Schlundt would lead the way in scoring with 33, followed by Leonard's 23 and Farley's 19, for a 91-to-79 win.

Indiana would use a 40-foot jump shot by Paul Poff in overtime to beat the Wildcats of Northwestern, 90 to 88. Indiana had now won 17 games in a row. The Hoosiers' dream of an undefeated Big Ten season would fall at Minneapolis, as the Gophers of Minnesota hit a shot with two seconds left to send the Hoosiers home in defeat, 65 to 63. The Mac Men had now lost three games on the season by a total of 5 points. Indiana would finish the Big Ten season at home with a win against Iowa, 68 to 61, behind Schlundt's 22. The Hoosiers had finished 17 and 1 in the Big Ten and 18 and 3 overall, and for the first time in school history ranked number one in the country.

During the season, Indiana set yet another record when Jack Wright of Richmond, Indiana, hit a free throw against Butler at Bloomington to give Indiana its first ever 100-point game. McCracken would finish the regular season, his twelfth at Indiana, with an overall record of 192 wins against just 62 defeats, and a Big Ten mark of 111 wins as compared to 47 defeats, and of course, his first Big Ten Championship.

Indiana would now head into its second NCAA tournament. Indiana would receive a first-round bye and take on the winner of the DePaul of Chicago/Miami of Ohio game. DePaul prevailed, and Indiana played DePaul of Chicago at Chicago Stadium, just a few miles from the Blue Demons' campus. Four of DePaul's five starters were from Chicago and averaged in height six-foot-three, compared to Indiana's starters who averaged six-foot-four. DePaul would enter the game with a record of 19 and 7, compared to Indiana's 19 and 3.

Indiana would be in the lead from the beginning of the game, but DePaul fought to stay close. Indiana's dynamic duo of Mr. Inside and Mr. Outside led the way for the Hoosiers. Schlundt would have 23 and Leonard would chip in 22, and Indiana would win a close one, 82 to 80. DePaul's Ray Meyer would say to Branch, "We threw everything we had at you, but it wasn't enough. You guys are too tough."[2] People at the game would agree with Meyer, saying that if this had been a hockey game, the penalty box would have been full all night. Meyer would say after the game that the Blue Demons were behind IU 100 per cent.

*Leonard scores over DePaul in NCAA tourney
as Dick Farley and Paul Poff look on.*

*Leonard, Farley, and Schlundt look for a call in NCAA game vs. DePaul.*

*Don Schlundt scores 2 of his 30 points against
Kansas in the '53 championship game.*

Next up for the Mac Men was Notre Dame. This was the same team
that had beaten Indiana the second game of the season by one point.
Indiana was ready to enact some revenge on the Irish. Indiana jumped
out to a 10-point halftime lead of 42 to 32. Indiana center Schlundt,
on his twenty first birthday was unstoppable on the day unstoppable on
the day, crushing the Irish with 13 field goals and 15 free throws for a
total of 41 points as Indiana cruised past the Irish, 79 to 66, to advance
in the tourney to face Louisiana State.

*Don Schlundt scores 2 of his 41 points over Notre Dame, March 14, 1953.*

*Branch with Don Schlundt on March 14, 1953, when Schlundt would break the Chicago stadium scoring record with 41 points.*

*McCracken presents Don Schlundt with his*
*Regional MVP award, March 14, 1953.*

During the NCAA regionals, the starting players for each team were individually introduced and a spotlight on the floor followed them just the way McCracken had it done at the IU Fieldhouse by the end of the regular season. When Schlundt was introduced, he was listed as six-foot-nine from South Bend, Indiana. After the championship game, McCracken was asked to present the Most Valuable Player Award. McCracken took out a slip of paper from his pocket and introduced "Don Schlundt of Washington Clay Township," noting that, "If Don here, a sophomore, continues to improve and if he works hard, he may turn out to be a pretty fair country ball-player before he's finished."[3] Branch McCracken's need to keep working to improve was on display for everyone to see. Schlundt would respond years later in a 1970 interview about Branch: "You take five individuals as smart aleck as probably we were back then. Well, you have to have a certain type of coach. I don't think there were any other coaches in the country that could have handled five young underclassmen as well as McCracken did. ... McCracken had a way of uniting the team, exploding when he had to, knocking our ears back when he had to, which we certainly needed back then, and just to be a father off the court to us and offer us advice."[4]

Indiana was now in Kansas City for the semifinal game. The same tournament manager from the 1940 tournament was still there, and he would tell Branch that people had always remembered the way Indiana had played, how much the people had enjoyed Indiana's running game, and that he felt Indiana's style of play had helped to make the tournament the popular success it was by 1953. This was a testament to McCracken's philosophy "that there is no substitute for speed."[5]

Indiana would come out in the game on fire, hitting on 14 of their first 16 shots to jump out to an 11-point lead, 31 to 20. LSU had started off the game clogging the middle to take away Schlundt, however, Leonard was making them pay by hitting his first six shots from outside. This opened up the middle as the Tigers had to jump out on Leonard, freeing Schlundt inside. Indiana would take an 8-point lead into the locker room at the half, 49 to 41. The Tigers were led by the great Bob Pettit, but the combination of Schlundt and Leonard would prove to be too much for them on this day as Indiana emerged victorious, 80 to 67. Schlundt ended the game with 29 points and Leonard added 22. LSU would be led by future Hall of Famer Bob Pettit's 29.

*Branch and the '53 champions prepare for a tourney sendoff.*

The stage was now set for a rematch of 1940's championship game between Indiana and host Kansas. The Kansas team would enter the game as the defending national champions. George Bolinger of the Bloomington Daily described the game in this manner: "Schlundt tallied 30 points including 9 of IU's 10 in the last period. But Bobby Leonard canned the winning free throw as well as 11 other points. Charlie Kraak turned in the greatest game of his career, when it was needed most. Burke Scott was a dervish all over the floor, and contributed six vital points early, and Dick Farley came up with his usual great but ensuing performance on both the offense and defense. A quartet of subs spelled the starters, especially when the threat of too many fouls got Indiana into trouble early in the game. And each Dick White, Phil Byers, Jim DeaKyne, and Paul Poff contributed a healthy share to a slim victory. The pressure was all on Indiana, the nation's number one team.

"The pressure would tell, too, on the Hoosiers as they would be assessed with three technical fouls for futile burst of temper over what Indiana would consider unjust decisions. Kansas would convert two technical fouls into points and receive possession of the ball twice, scoring baskets each time. But when all of the returns were in, it was Indiana on top by a small but ever so final margin of one point. The score would be tied 14 different times. Indiana had the lead 10 times and the Jayhawks were in front 9 times. Indiana's largest lead was three while the Hoosiers would trail by as much as six. Kraak would surprise the Jayhawks with his offensive work as he would put in 12 first half points. Working with finesse beneath the basket, he scored a lay-up and two tip ins and added six points from the free throw line in drawing Kansas into five different fouls. Leonard absolutely thrilled everyone in the auditorium with a last second shot from mid-floor that zipped through the net as the horn sounded."[6] Kelly of Kansas would make the all-tourney team because of his defensive work on Bobby Leonard; however, it would be Kelly that fouled Leonard with 27 seconds left. Leonard's shot would almost go in, teasing around the rim before falling off. He would, however, be awarded two free throws. Leonard would miss the first but hit the second to give Indiana a 1-point lead, 69 to 68. Indiana would then pressure Kansas all the way for the last 27 seconds and force a desparate shot that would not go in, and the Hoosiers were national champs, 69 to 68. During the game, Kansas leading scorer B.H. Born would be assessed his fifth foul; however, Phog Allen argued it was only his fourth. After much discussion, the officials said it was only four fouls on Born, at which point McCracken exploded, saying, "You had five on him and you changed it to four. You know you did. We came out here and are supposed to be your guest. You're robbing us."[7]

To understand what a McCracken explosion looked like, it needs only to be described by Tug Wilson in his book, *The Big Ten*: "Anytime a dubious foul was called against one of his Indiana University cagers, Branch emitted a sound like a steam calliope gone amok, and then exploded off the bench straight up, to a consistent height of 9 feet 4 ½ inches (verified by no less than three official observers as required by Irate Basketball Coach-Watchers rule)."[8] Despite Branch's objections, Born remained in the game with four fouls.

After the game, reporters came to Leonard after talking to McCracken and told Leonard that McCracken said Bobby had ice water in his veins. Leonard replied, "If that was ice water, it sure felt warm running down my leg."[9]

*Branch and the '53 Hoosiers celebrate Indiana and Branch's second national championship (Don Schlundt, 34; Charlie Kraak, 13; and Bob Leonard, in back ground).*

*McCracken with his 1953 championship team (L–R, Phil Byers, Goethe Chambers, James Deakyne, Dick Farley, Charlie Kraak, Bobby Leonard, Branch McCracken, Paul Poff, Don Schlundt, Jim Schooley, Burke Scott, Dick White, Jack Wright, and Ryan Fifer).*

*National champions (L–R, Dick Farley, Phil Byers, Dick White, Don Schlundt, Jim Deakyne, Ernie Andres, Goethe Chambers, Bobby Leonard, Branch McCracken, Charlie Kraak, Jack Wright, Jim Schooley, and Ron Fifer).*

*McCracken celebrating the national championshop (L–R, Charlie Kraak, Bobby Leonard, Branch McCracken, Don Schlundt, Paul Poff, and Jim Schooley).*

The result remained: Indiana had gone to Kansas City twice to face Kansas for the national championship and twice had returned to Bloomington the conquering heroes. McCracken had told his team after their second victory over Illinois, "I never praise you fellows, and sometimes you must think I'm pretty hard. I criticize and tell you where you do the wrong things and leave the praise to your mothers and sweethearts and friends. But tonight, I'll have to say that you're the greatest team in the country."[10]

Bobby Leonard, the captain of the team, would say, "It was one of those ball clubs where everybody just fit together like a glove, everybody did. I think the thing was, there was no jealousy, no nothing, we went out with a team concept. I don't think I have ever been with a group of guys in my life that we were as close to each other as that ball club. That was a great basketball team."[11]

Jim Schooley would echo Leonard's thoughts. "There was no jealousy on that team. We all liked each other. Mac knew he had special talent in Leonard and Schlundt, but he made us into a team. Mac would get everyone involved. It was the big guys' job to get the rebound and look to the side to get the ball out so we could run and get the lay-ups. He used to say 'treat that ball like a hot potato. Go, go, go, run, run, and run.'"

McCracken would win his second National Coach of the Year Award. Leonard would be All-American, All-Final Four, All-Big Ten first team. Schlundt would be All-American, All-Final Four, All Big Ten first team, and Big Ten MVP. Schlundt would score 123 points in four NCAA games for a 30.8 average. He would also set a free throw record, hitting 49 to best Kansas's Lovellette's 35 from the year before. Branch and the team would travel to New York to be on Ed Sullivan's "Toast of the Town" after the '53 Championship.

*McCracken riding in downtown Bloomington with the championship team.*

*Branch ties championship banner on the car for the victory parade, 1953.*

As a team, Indiana's 23 wins would be the most ever under a McCracken-coached team. They set a record of 108 free throws, breaking the 80 by Illinois the previous year. Indiana's total of 310 points also would set a record for most points in four games in the tourney.

Not only would McCracken give the Hoosiers their second NCAA Championship, but he would also save the day for one particular Indiana fan. In this magical season, Branch would help make it even more magical for one Indiana student, a person named Charles Cogan from Clinton, Indiana. Cogan was in the Old Fieldhouse one fall day, watching the hardwood floor being put down. Standing next to him was a tall gentleman with full white hair. Charles commented on how big the court was. The gentleman shared how much he enjoyed watching the court being assembled each year. As he left, his friends gave him a hard time about knowing such a famous person. Charles was puzzled as to what they meant until they explained that the man he had been talking too was none other than Branch McCracken. Charles would from that point on strike up a distant friendship with the legendary coach. When the two would pass by each other on campus, they would wave and say hi. As the season wore on, the Hoosiers would find themselves in the NCAA Championship. Charles and his friends decided at the last minute to go to the game, making the trip to Kansas City. Like many college students making a last-minute decision, they left with very little money. Arriving in Kansas City, Charles found it his job to get the tickets for the game. Going to the on-site IU ticket office, he discovered that the ticket manager could not take a personal check unless it was countersigned by an IU representative. Undaunted, Charles asked if Coach McCracken was in that very hotel. Told yes, but that he would not sign the check, Charles went to McCracken's room anyway. Coach McCracken would answer the door himself wearing a T-shirt and baggy boxer shorts. It was apparent he had been resting before the game. Charles explained his situation to McCracken, and Branch countersigned the check. Charles thanked the coach and promised to cheer on the Hoosiers that night. Going back to the ticket manager,

Charles showed him the countersigned check. "You got Branch McCracken to countersign your check?" Charles would answer, "Of course. I knew he would remember me."[12] McCracken had saved the day for Charles and many other students and fans of Indiana basketball. 1953 would be a year for the ages.

*Branch with Big Ten commissioner Tug Wilson after Indiana's second national championship, March 17, 1953.*

# Chapter 13

## THE '54 SEASON: CHAMPIONS BACK-TO-BACK

*Branch is featured on the Indianapolis News record book after the '53 championship (Indianapolis News).*

The year was 1953. The Hoosiers would begin the '53–54 campaign as national champions as well as Big Ten champions. The '52–53 season had witnessed Branch ending his long string of seven second-place finishes in the Big Ten, having started his coaching career at Indiana with six straight.

*Branch McCracken looks out on the old fieldhouse as he prepares to defend Indiana's national title, November 4, 1953.*

The Hoosiers would start the season ranked number one with two returning All-Americans in Don Schlundt and Bobby Leonard. The Hoosiers would also be bolstered with the return of the other three starters from the '53 championship team. Coach McCracken would address the expectations and pressures that came with being the defending national champions that would return the entire starting lineup for another season: "We're really on the spot this year. People figure that with the same bunch we had last year we should breeze through. It's not that simple, and a lot of things can happen. The Big Ten is much tougher from top to bottom this year than last. Add to that the fact that everyone is going to be pointing at us and that the pressure is going to be on us from the start to finish."[1]

Indiana would start the season on December 5 with a 78-to-65 victory over Cincinnati behind Schlundt and Leonard's 20 points apiece. Next came Kansas State, and the Hoosiers would earn their second win to open the season with a 92-to 66-pounding of the Wildcats. Big Don Schlundt would provide the Hoosiers with 25 points in the win.

A trip to Butler produced a third win for the Hoosiers as McCracken played fifteen players in a 76-to-57 win after opening the first half with a 36-to-16 advantage. Notre Dame would come to Bloomington still smarting from their loss to Indiana in the tourney the previous year. The Irish would triple team Schlundt, who had burned them for 41 points in the tourney. This, of course, opened up the outside for Leonard, who took advantage of just such an opening to torch the Irish for 21 in a 66-to-55 Hoosier victory.

Indiana would then go on the road for three games. The Hoosiers, minus Leonard, who was sitting out the game due to a shoulder injury, defeated Montana by 20. Next, Indiana played at Corvallis, Oregon, and beat number 11 Oregon State, 76 to 72, behind Schlundt's 34 points. In a situation that occurred back then but that would seem strange to college basketball fans of today, Indiana would play Oregon State again the next night on the same court. This time, Oregon State's seven-foot center, Wade Halbrook, would score 21 points, and Oregon State defeated number one Indiana by 16, 67 to 51.

Indiana was now ready to start the Big Ten portion of their season. They would open on the road at Ann Arbor, Michigan, and behind Schlundt's 30 and Leonard's 21 points, Indiana would win a close one, 62 to 60. The Badgers of Wisconsin invaded Bloomington, and Indiana escaped with a 3-point win led by Schlundt, who would account for 29 of Indiana's points. Indiana would next go to Minnesota, the site of their only loss in 18 Big Ten games last year. Indiana would get a balanced scoring attack with four players in double figures to avenge their loss last year with a 71-to-63 victory.

Purdue came to Indiana next, and in what had become a very common occurrence, Schlundt would again lead Indiana in scoring with 30 points on 9 field goals and 12 free throws. The Hoosiers would send the Boilermakers home in defeat, 73 to 67. Indiana would dispatch two more Big Ten foes in Wisconsin and Ohio State before venturing out of the conference and defeating the Louisville Cardinals, 80 to 71. The

Hoosiers yet again relied on the power combination of Schlundt and Leonard for scoring with 29 and 19. The Hoosiers would win two more games in conference before taking on the Wildcats of Northwestern in Evanston, Illinois. Northwestern would shock Indiana and the rest of the Big Ten with a 100-to-90 overtime win over Indiana, giving the Hoosiers their second loss of the season and first in Big Ten play.

Indiana was now tied with the Iowa Hawkeyes for the Big Ten lead and would go to West Lafayette to play Purdue on February 15. Nothing made Branch happier then beating Purdue, and the Hoosiers were about to make Branch a very happy man. The Hoosiers rolled over Purdue by 36 points, 86 to 50. Indiana would then go on to beat Michigan State by 2 at East Lansing. In seven days Indiana had played three games, all on the road, and McCracken could see the signs of fatigue

On February 22, Iowa visited Bloomington and walked away with an 86-to-64 victory. McCracken would comment on the Hoosiers and the drain the season and its pressures had taken a toll on his ball club: "This team is tired, not as much physically as mentally. Every team we've met has pointed for us and gone all out against us. The constant strain of meeting that challenge every night and getting ourselves up for it is showing its effects."[2]

Indiana would bounce back and win games against Ohio State and Illinois, the latter being significant in that a loss to Illinois would have enabled Illinois to tie Indiana for the Big Ten championship and sent Illinois to the NCAA tourney. The Hoosiers, however, prevailed and claimed their second straight Big Ten Title.

The first round of the tourney would be played in Iowa City against number 5 Notre Dame, a team the Hoosiers had already defeated this season and the team Indiana beat last year in the tourney on their way to the NCAA Championship. This time, however, Indiana did not play their best basketball, and it would cost them dearly. Again the Irish would triple team Schlundt as they had in the previous contest that year, but this time the rest of the Hoosier team could not score from outside as they had in the earlier encounter.

Despite all of what would unfold in the game, the Hoosiers still had a chance to pull it out in the end. Dick White would recall, "I remember Leonard was put back into the game for the last play and scored a layup for what looked like the winning points, but he was called for charging into

Dick Rosenthal, and we lost a chance for a second straight title."[3] Leonard would add, "I drove for the layup and scored, but was called for charging. My points counted, but Rosenthal was given two free throws and he made them. That was the game. I'll never forget that loss. We had such a great team. Of course Notre Dame was a basketball power then, as well. They had an outstanding team, but we had beaten them in the regular season and I still feel we had a better team."[4] Leonard would say even today that he felt as if that game was for the national title even though Notre Dame would lose their next contest. With the 65-to-64 loss to the Irish, the Hoosiers' hopes for a second straight national title were crushed.

McCracken would say following the game that Notre Dame had played a great game and were deserving of the win, but this defeat was very hard to take because "I don't think any basketball team in history has had a more loyal following, and I wanted to win for them more than anyone else."[5]

Indiana would end McCracken's second Big Ten championship season on a high note, so to speak, with a 73-to-62 consolation game victory over Louisiana State. Bobby Leonard would end his illustrious career at Indiana with an 8-point performance. Both Leonard and Schlundt would be selected as first team All-Big Ten and All-Americans. Indiana would finish with their second straight season with 20 or more wins and would be ranked fourth in the nation.

*Branch McCracken with Bobby Leonard, 1953.*

# Chapter 14

## THE '55 AND '56 SEASONS: SIXTH PLACE

Aᴌᴌ-Aᴍᴇʀɪᴄᴀɴ Dᴏɴ Sᴄʜᴌᴜɴᴅᴛ ᴀɴᴅ ꜰᴏᴜʀ-ʏᴇᴀʀ sᴛᴀʀᴛᴇʀ Burke Scott would return for their final year in an Indiana uniform to play for McCracken. In three seasons, the two seniors had led McCracken's Indiana Hoosiers to a record of 59 wins against just 13 defeats. McCracken and the Hoosiers had already seen the departure of All-American Bobby Leonard, Dick Farley, and Charlie Kraak. McCracken would address the media and say simply that the Hoosiers didn't figure to be any more than respectable this year.

The year before, Indiana had finished 20 and 4, winning their second straight undisputed Big Ten title. Indiana would return Wally Choice and Dick Neal, with the addition of 1953 Indiana High School Mr. Basketball Hallie Bryant out of Indianapolis's Crispus Attucks High School.

Indiana would open the '54–55 season against Valparaiso in Bloomington, Indiana. Wally Choice would account for 29 points for the Hoosiers, while All-American Don Schlundt opened his senior season with 20 points. Missouri would come into Bloomington two nights later and walk away with a 3-point victory, 64 to 61, despite Schlundt's 25-point effort.

Indiana would go on the road to South Bend and hand the Irish their first loss at home in 23 games. Sophomore Hallie Bryant hit a corner jumper with 44 seconds left to give Indiana a 69 to 68 lead, and the Mac Men would go on to win 73 to 70. Indiana's record would now read 2 and 1 in this young season.

Southern Methodist would travel east to Bloomington, and despite Schlundt's amazing 41-point performance, the Methodists would walk away with an 83-to-78 win. The Hoosiers hit the road for games in Cincinnati, Ohio; Manhattan, Kansas; and St. Louis, Missouri. The Hoosiers would drop all three games. Indiana lost the Cincinnati game by 32 points, 97 to 65, for the worst defeat since losing to DePaul of Chicago, 81 to 43, while McCracken was still in the navy.

Indiana would stop the losing streak at four by defeating Michigan, 95 to 77, in Bloomington, behind Schlundt's 30 and Scott's 19. Indiana then traveled to Illinois and began another losing streak that would climb to three with losses to Illinois, 99 to 75, Minnesota, 88 to 74, and Wisconsin, 77 to 66.

Thankfully, Indiana would return home to a Fieldhouse that proved to be very friendly to Mac's players, as the host Hoosiers entertained the Spartans of Michigan State. Although the Spartans would hold a commanding 51-to-36 halftime lead, Indiana, under McCracken leadership, would go on a 20-to-3 run to stop the bleeding and win going away, 88 to 77, behind Schlundt's 36 points. Choice would add 16 for good measure.

Butler came to Bloomington and the Mac Men ran Butler back to Indianapolis, 87 to 56, behind Schlundt's 23 and Choice's 20. On the fifth of February, Indiana traveled to Columbus, Ohio, to take on the Ohio State Buckeyes. Indiana would lose a second-half 12-point lead to lose to Ohio State by 3.

Indiana beat Wisconsin at home, 65 to 58. Indiana would then go on another three-game losing streak to Iowa, Minnesota, and Northwestern. With four games remaining, two of them against rival Purdue, the Hoosiers managed a split outcome. Indiana hosted Purdue in Bloomington and won their thirteenth straight against Purdue, 75 to 62. Wally Choice poured in 29 followed by Schlundt's 19. Five days later, Purdue would stop the streak and gain a measure of revenge with a 92-to-67 win over the Hoosiers.

Indiana's last road game would be at Michigan State, and the Spartans would win, 93 to 77. The Hoosiers closed out the season with a win against the Buckeyes of Ohio State at home, 84 to 66. Schlundt would end his brilliant career with a 47-point performance, hitting 11 field goals and 25 free throws on 30 attempts for his third consecutive scoring title, and finishing as the all-time leading scorer in Big Ten history, as well as IU history, with 2,192 points. Schlundt would also be named All-American for the third time. Indiana would finish the season with only McCracken's second losing season. Students, concerned that the Big Bear might not come back, would meet about 5,000 strong at McCracken's home to show both their love and support for the Indiana legend.

The '56 season would be the second straight second division finish in the Big Ten for Coach McCracken and his Indiana Hoosiers. The

Hoosiers would miss three-time All-American Don Schlundt, along with fellow starter Burke Scott, another member of the '53 national championship team. Senior captain Wally Choice would return, as would junior Hallie Bryant, and the season would unveil much-anticipated debut of sophomore Archie Dees.

Indiana opened at home against Ohio with a 93-to-74 victory. Dees would debut with 21 points, and a preview of what was to come for the next three years would be revealed. Dees's 21 and Bryant's 23 would power Indiana to a 2 and 0 beginning on the season, with a 96-to-72 win over Kansas State. The Billekens of St. Louis would invade Bloomington and go back west to St. Louis with an 86-to-75 win over Indiana. Indiana hit the road against Missouri, and behind players scoring in double figures, led by Choice's 19, would come away with an 81-to-78 win. Indiana exacted a measure of revenge against the Bearcats of Cincinnati, 80 to 61, as Hallie Bryant poured in 31 points for the Hoosiers. Indiana would win their next four contests against Drake, Butler, Northwestern, and Wisconsin. Wally Choice would lead the Hoosiers in scoring for the four contests with an average of 23 points a game.

Indiana would go to Minnesota and sustain a 6-point loss. Illinois visited Bloomington and destroyed the Hoosiers, 96 to 72, despite Dees giving Indiana a 22-point effort. Indiana would win their next two games against Michigan State and Notre Dame by scores of 79 to 70 and 81 to 76, remembering that McCracken liked to schedule a nonconference game after semester break.

Next, the Mac Men would go to Columbus and lose, 100 to 82, invoking the story told earlier in this chapter. Remember, McCracken just didn't like to lose. You could say it wasn't in his DNA. Indiana lost its second game in a row, 92 to 89, to Illinois. Dees would score 25 in that game, followed by 20 from Choice and 17 from Bryant. The hosting Hoosiers would beat Michigan, 97 to 73. Indiana then fell to Wisconsin despite Wally Choice's 27-point performance.

Indiana would then split their next two games. They lost to Iowa despite three Hoosiers scoring 20 points or more, with Choice leading the way with 24, followed by Dees's and Thompson's 20. Iowa held on to win, 87 to 83. Indiana would travel to Northwestern and escape with a 2-point win, 84 to 82, with five players in double figures, again led by sophomore Archie Dees with 22.

Indiana finished the season losing their last two, falling to Purdue, 73 to 71, and closing the season on the road with an 84-to-73 loss to the Iowa Hawkeyes. Choice would close his career at Indiana hitting on 10 field goals and 5 free throws for a total of 25 points. McCracken's Hoosiers would finish with a winning record of 13 wins against 9 defeats, although they would finish sixth in the Big Ten for the second year in a row.

# Chapter 15

# THE '56–57 SEASON: THE THIRD CHAMPIONSHIP

INDIANA WOULD ENTER THE '56–57 SEASON COMING OFF TWO SEASONS in which they would finish tied for sixth in the Big Ten, with records of 8 and 14 and 13 and 9, respectively. This would represent the second worst finish in the Big Ten for a McCracken-coached Indiana team in his 16 years at the helm of IU. The '54–55 team's 8 and 14 season would represent only the second time in McCracken's first 15 years that his team would suffer through a losing season. To give a proper perspective of how rare the '55 year had been to both McCracken and Indiana, McCracken would end his coaching career with only three losing seasons in 24 years at IU.

The Hoosiers would return four starters from the '55–56 season that had produced McCracken's fourteenth winning season as head coach at IU. Besides the four returning starters, four other lettermen would return, giving the Mac Men as they were called an experienced crew with which to work.

McCracken announced before the season to the press, "I'm not predicting where we'll finish, but we plan to have a lot of say concerning the outcome of the race. ... This is going to be one of our better running ball clubs, I think it will be the fastest since our '51 club and with considerably more size."[1] The '51 club had finished with a record of 19 wins and 3 losses, finishing second in the Big Ten with a conference mark of 12 and 2, and were led by the wonderful All-American from Shelbyville, Indiana, Bill Garrett. It should be noted that Garrett would be the last six-foot-three All-American center, testifying to his great basketball ability. Indiana football great All-American and Hall of Famer George Taliaferro would call Bill Garrett his generation's "Michael Jordan."[2] The tallest member of the '51 team was six-foot-five Don Luft, who would later become an assistant coach for the Hoosiers. In contrast, the '56–57 team would list six players who stood over six-foot-five and five others who would match Garrett's height at six-foot-three.

The Hoosiers opened the '56–57 campaign on the fourth of December in Bloomington with a 64-57 win over Valparaiso. All-American center Archie Dees would score 28 points, grab 25 rebounds. and reject 6 of the Crusaders' shots to lead the Hoosiers to victory. Guard forward Pete Obremskey would knock down four shots and connect on three free throws to become the only other Hoosier in double figures on that night with 11.

Four days later in Bloomington in front of 7,500 fans, Dees would score 28 and Obremskey would add 16 while Eugene Flowers contributed 11 as Indiana rolled past Southern Illinois, 80 to 57. Next up were the Butler Bulldogs, who invaded Bloomington on December 10 to push the Hoosiers to the max in a closely contested match that would see Indiana prevail, 73 to 68. Archie Dees would, for the third straight time, lead Indiana in scoring with 24 points on 11 field goals and two free throws. Jerry Thompson and Charlie Hodson would join Dees in double figures with 14 and 11 points, respectively. Butler's famed Bobby Plump would add 18 in a losing effort for the visiting Bulldogs. This would complete an impressive three-game home sweep in just seven days. The student newspaper would talk about Indiana's fast-breaking brand of basketball with a squad, as they put it, "that had speed to burn in Pete Obremskey, Charlie Hodson, Archie Dees, Dick Neal, Jerry Thompson, and Hallie Bryant."[3]

On the fifteenth of December, the Mac men would visit 14-ranked Kansas State and suffer a heartbreaking 84-to-77 loss in overtime. Indiana would stay on the road, traveling to Philadelphia to play at the Palestra. The Hoosiers would play in a doubleheader against both LaSalle and Villanova on December 18 and 20. Indiana's Mac Men won the opener of the doubleheader against LaSalle, 93 to 80, led by Archie Dees's 31-point and 18-rebound outburst. Hallie Bryant would add 16 points and Jerry Thompson would connect on 7 baskets for a total of 17 points. Two nights later, it was Indiana's turn to face Villanova. Villanova placed one guard on the top and then jammed up the middle with a 1-2-2 zone that effectively held Archie Dees to just 3 baskets and a career-low of 8 points. Thompson's 16, Bryant's 10, and Obremskey's 12 were not enough, and the Hoosiers would fall by 10 to the Wildcats, 79 to 69.

Four days after Christmas on December 29, McCracken's old friend Johnny Wooden would bring his UCLA Bruins, the school Mac had turned down years earlier, to Bloomington and walk away with a 52-to-48 win in a contest that was described as an ugly game, marred by poor shooting on the part of both sides.

The Big Ten season would open at home for Indiana on January the fifth as Michigan came calling. The Hoosiers proved to be inhospitable host, handing the Wolverines a 73-to-68 loss as Dees paved the way with 26 points, followed by Dick Neal with 22. Two days later, Wisconsin would come to Bloomington and encounter the trio of Dees, Thompson, and Neal as they would account for 28, 12, and 10 points in leading the Hoosiers to a 79-to-68 victory.

*Big Ten MVP Archie Dees scores over Michigan*

The Hoosiers would next embark on a four-game road trip, with its first stop in West Lafayette, where Lamar Lundy would match Dees's point total, each with 15. The Hoosiers would lose their first one on the road, 70 to 64. Next up, the Hoosiers would have four men in double figures, led by Archie Dees with 28; however, the Hoosiers lost their second road game in a row in a shootout with Illinois, 112 to 91

Indiana would travel to South Bend and lose a third game in a row, 94 to 82. The defeat would drop Indiana to a 500 record at 6 and 6. Indiana had not just suffered their third straight loss, but would lose a few players to academic ineligibility. Indiana's season looked very much in danger of getting away from them. A trip to Iowa City seemed to provide a cure as

Indiana prevailed over the Hawkeyes, 82 to 66. The Hoosiers hit Iowa with a balanced scoring attack. Neal and Hodson would each throw in 21 points while Dees would go for 18 and Bryant for 17.

Back home again in Indiana, the Mac Men defeated Northwestern in front of 8,000 rabid fans, 74 to 56. On February ninth, the Buckeyes of Ohio State would play the Hoosiers in front of 10,000 screaming fans and leave town on the short end of a 69-to-59 score from another very balanced scoring attack. The Hoosiers were led by Dees's 17, Bryant's 16, Neal's 15, Obremskey's 12, and Hodson's 9.

On February the eleventh, with another 10,000 fans in the stands, Archie Dees would pour in 29 points, backed by Neal's 24, and the Mac Men would dispatch the Gophers, 91 to 72, for their fourth straight win.

The Hoosiers would next travel to Evanston and down the Wildcats by 13 with three players scoring in the 20s. Bryant would lead the way with 24; Dees and Neal would both add 22. Back in Bloomington, All-American Archie Dees would go off for 37 points on 15 field goals and 7 free throws. Indiana would beat the Hawkeyes for the second time in 16 days. The Hoosiers would venture into Madison, Wisconsin, and defeat the Badgers, 85 to 74, for their seventh straight win to move their Big Ten mark to 9 wins and 2 defeats, which would push Indiana into tenth place in the Associated Press Poll. Indiana would travel to Ann Arbor to face Michigan, the first Big Ten team they had faced and defeated this season, only to lose a heartbreaker, 87 to 86. All-American Dees was doing everything in his power to give the Hoosiers a victory, hitting on 15 field goals and scoring 39 points, but it just wasn't enough.

A date with Michigan State at East Lansing loomed ahead for the Hoosiers in what would shape up to be a battle for first place. The Spartans led nearly the entire contest and remained in front for a glorious 76-to-61 victory over IU. The Hoosiers were again led in scoring by Dees with 28. Indiana had one game to go, hosting Illinois at home on the fourth day of March. The seniors would go out in style, as Neal, Hodson, and Bryant would score 12, 17, and 15 points, respectively, and junior Archie Dees would throw in 25 just for good measure.

Indiana would tie for the Big Ten title with their 84-to-76 win over Illinois. Indiana and Michigan State would both stand atop the Big Ten rankings with 10 and 4 marks. By virtue of the fact that Indiana had gone the previous year to the tourney in 1954 as Big Ten champs, the automatic berth would be given to the Michigan State. However, Branch McCracken had secured his third Big Ten championship and the Hoosiers, under McCracken, were back on top where they belonged.

Branch would reflect back on the team and the season that had given him his third Big Ten championship in the next year's Indiana Media Guide: "A coach feels fortunate if two or three times over the season he can key a squad to play better than it has any real right to play. Last year's squad had an unusual ability to get itself up for a game. I'd say we played seven games last season in which we played over our heads, or at least up to our very peak."[4]

McCracken's Hoosiers would finish the year 14 and 8, with Archie Dees awarded the Big Ten MVP award and being named All-American.

# Chapter 16

# THE '57–58 SEASON: THE LAST TITLE

THE 1957–58 SEASON WOULD BRING BRANCH HIS FOURTH AND LAST Big Ten Title. The team and the season would be described in the '58 Arbutus in this fashion: "The 1958 version of the "Hurry'n Hoosiers" under the dynamic coaching of Branch McCracken, caught fire in mid-season and went on to burn a path all the way to the Big Ten Championship."[1] This was McCracken's fourth triumph in the last six years.

As the season started, there was little doubt as to the makeup of the front line: on hand at center was All-American Archie Dees, while at forward post hard-charging Pete Obremskey and sharp-shooting Jerry Thompson led the way. The Hoosiers would have a tall sophomore, Frank Radovich, to come off the bench to add relief in the front court if any were needed. Ray Pavy would comment years later, "People just don't remember how really, really good Radovich was."[2]

It was at the backcourt spots that McCracken had cause for concern. After much experimentation, McCracken would come up with what he felt was the right combination in senior guard Sam Gee and sophomore guard Bob Wilkinson. Both guards would develop into good shots and were consistently harassing opposing dribblers with their flypaper nearness. The winning quintet, which went on the propel Indiana into the NCAA regionals, would gain valuable bench strength from the likes of Jim Hinds, Allen Schlegelmilch, and Ray Ball.

McCracken gave this assessment of the '58 Hoosiers before the start of the season: "How can anyone figure that we'll be as good or better than we were last year beats me. We lost three starters. One, Dick Neal at forward, was the sparkplug who got us going and shot so well he set a new conference percentage record. The other two, Hallie Bryant and Charlie Hodson, were our regular guards and contributed just as heavily to our success. ... Those three boys were our second-, third-, and fourth-ranking scorers, accounting for more than 45 percent of the points we scored. You just don't reach down and pull our replacements of that same caliber like rabbits out of a hat."[3]

So what were the possibilities for the '58 team to become Branch's fourth Big Ten Championship team? Branch would reluctantly address that by saying, "If everything works out as we would like it, it could be a real good team, but we have to prove it and it's not fair to the squad to expect too much of it without justification."[67]

The Mac Men would return the Big Ten's Most Valuable Player for the '57 season and its conference scoring champion in Archie Dees. Branch had devised a plan to move Archie out of the post to a forward position to make room for six-foot-seven Frank Radovich from Hammond, Indiana, in the center position for the Hoosiers.

The '58 season would start on a sour note when McCracken's Hoosiers lost the home opener to Ohio University by a score of 76 to 68, despite the scoring up front of Archie Dees with 24 and newcomer Frank Radovich's 21 before a crowd of 10,000. Kansas State would be the second opponent for the Hoosiers at home, and again the Mac Men would fall before another crowd of 10,000 by a score of 66 to 61 as the Wildcats held Dees to 17 on the night. The Hoosiers traveled to Columbia, Missouri, where the Tigers, despite Dees' 30 points, would give the Hoosiers their third straight defeat. This would be the first time in 28 years that an Indiana team had started a season with three straight losses.

Indiana hosted Saint Mary's of California and, with four men in double figures, get their first win of the year and break their three-game losing streak, 79 to 66. Oregon State would travel to Bloomington on December 23 and start another Hoosier losing streak by defeating Indiana, 62 to 51, allowing Dees 25 while holding the other nine Hoosier players to just 26 total points. Indiana would travel up Highway 37 to Indianapolis to take on the Butler Bulldogs. Butler would place five players in double figures, led by Cox and Plump with 19 and 17, respectively, while the Hoosiers would get 30 points from Dees and 18 from Thompson, losing to Butler, 84 to 78. The next day, the Hoosiers would take on the Notre Dame Fighting Irish. The Hoosiers were beaten, 89 to 74, and would see their season record slip to an un-Hoosier-like 1 and 6.

Northwestern would be the first Big Ten opponent for Indiana. The Wildcats came to Bloomington on January 4. Branch would go with just 6 players, one of those being little-used Sam Gee, who would make the offense move that day. Branch would see four of the six players score in double figures, and Indiana would start the Big Ten season on the right note with a 68-to-65 win.

Indiana traveled next to West Lafayette, and although Archie Dees torched the Boilers for 12 field goals and 14 free throws for 38 points, Purdue escaped with a 2-point victory by scoring the final 4 points of the contest. Indiana would be back in Bloomington for their next game, and Dees and Obremskey lit up the scoreboard with 26 and 23 points, but little Sam Gee hit 11 of 12 free throws for 15 total points to lead the Mac Men to an upset victory over the Fighting Illini by a score of 89 to 82. Gee would keep up his point contribution with 14 points as both Thompson and Dees would add 22 apiece for an Indiana 19-point victory over Minnesota. Indiana's win would make the Hoosiers 3 and 1 in the conference and put them in a tie with Michigan. Five days later, despite Dees's 33, the Hoosiers would lose by 4 to Iowa.

On February 3 at Minneapolis, the Hoosiers would drop to 3 and 3 in conference play with a 3-point loss to Minnesota. Indiana would then reel off two straight wins over Michigan State, 82 to 79, again using only six players (with five in double figures), and Wisconsin, 93 to 87.

Ohio State would come to Bloomington and defeat the Hoosiers by 10, 93 to 83, on Indiana's home court. Indiana's Big Ten record now stood at 5 wins and 4 losses. There were just five games remaining on the conference schedule, and the season for the Mac Men would hang in the balance for the opportunity to make something great happen.

On February 22, the Hoosiers traveled to Ohio State, and with Dees playing like the All American he was with 33 points and 19 boards, the Hoosiers would return the favor and defeat the Buckeyes, 88 to 83, proving that for either team in this series, on this season, at least 83 points in a game would not be enough.

Michigan would come to Bloomington and started off well with a 50-to-36 halftime lead. The very intense McCracken would peel paint off the locker room walls at halftime, but the point would be made to the team, and Indiana outscored in the second half by a score of 59 to 38 for a final tally that read, 95 to 88, and an IU win. On March 1, upstate rival Purdue would visit Bloomington, and the Hoosiers, behind Dees's 37, would avenge that 2-point loss from earlier in the season with a 14-point winner, 109 to 95.

The final two regular-season games were road contests at Illinois and Michigan State. Behind Dees's 33 and four other Hoosiers in double figures, the Mac Men would win by 10, 96 to 86. The final regular season game would be at Michigan State, and the winner would be the outright Big Ten champ and ticketed for a trip to the NCAA tournament. Reserve guard Bob Wilkinson led the Hoosiers in scoring with 18 points, including the final five points of the game, all from the free throw line. Gee would add 17, with Dees adding 14 and Thompson 11, as Indiana captured its fourth and last Big Ten Championship under Branch McCracken by a score of 75 to 72.

The Hoosiers would travel to Lexington, Kentucky, to play Notre Dame. Notre Dame would come out on fire in the game, and despite Dees's 28, Obremskey's 18, and Wilkinson's 17, IU would be no match this day for the Fighting Irish as the Hoosiers' hope in the NCAA were dashed, 94 to 87. The following night, Indiana would defeat Ohio, 98 to 91, in the consolation game of the tournament.

This would be, as mentioned earlier, Branch's final Big Ten championship and his fourth in six years. Archie Dees would win his second Big Ten MVP award and become the first player in the Big Ten to do so. Dees would finish the season with a 25.5 scoring average.

*Branch with two time Big Ten MVP Archie Dees*

# Chapter 17

# 1960 AND WHAT MIGHT HAVE BEEN

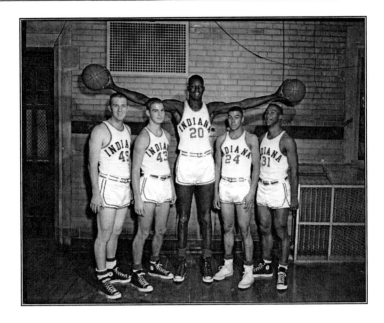

*Walt Bellamy with freshmen*

THE '59 SEASON HAD BEEN AN EVEN ONE. THE HOOSIERS WOULD FINISH fifth in the Big Ten with a 7 and 7 record, a reflection of the entire season, which saw Indiana finish with a 500 record of 11 and 11. However, the '59 season had witnessed a continuation of McCracken bringing in a great center to support the Hoosier cause. It had started in the late forties with Shelbyville's Bill Garrett, who at six-foot-three was the last of the great small centers. McCracken would then add Big Don Schlundt from South Bend Clay. Following Schlundt, who was himself a three time All-American, would be Mount Carmel of Illinois's Archie Dees, who would become the first two-time MVP of the Big Ten. Now on the stage would be Walt Bellamy of New Bern, North Carolina. Bellamy was truly a very special player, who would in his sophomore year lead Indiana in scoring at 17.4 per game and rebounding at 15.2 per game.

The 1960 season would be one that, played in a different era, might well have produced a very different result. The 1960 Indiana team, if allowed to participate in the NCAA tournament as the Big Ten runner-up as it would be allowed to today, might very well have produced

McCracken's third national championship. McCracken would return a team that, in his own words, "on a given night, could have beaten any club in the country, but on other nights they would have had trouble with almost anyone."[1] McCracken would say that what he was looking for foremost in this team was consistency.

The Mac Men possessed an imposing front court, starting of course with six-foot-eleven Walt Bellamy. Bellamy would be flanked on either side by six-foot-seven Frank Radovich from Hammond, Indiana, who as a senior would serve as the 1960 team captain, and six-foot-six Charley Hall from Terre Haute, Indiana. In 1959, Radovich had averaged 12.5 points a game and 10 rebounds a game. The backcourt would see five-eleven junior playmaker Herbie Lee from South Bend, who had averaged 13.6 points a game the previous year, and senior guard Bob Wilkinson from LA Porte, Indiana, whose leadership skills would run the team. McCracken's desire for this team was to play together as a team and show a desire to win like no other.

*Walt Bellamy with Branch*

Indiana started the season on the proper note, blasting Ball State by 40, resulting in a 103-to-63 victory. Big Bell would lead the way with 19 points as all fourteen players that played that day for McCracken would score. Indiana would next travel to Columbus, Missouri, on December 7. The Hoosiers trailed at the half, 43 to 38. They would mount a charge to pull within one in the closing minutes, but fall to the Tigers by three, 79 to 76. Senior Radovich would score 22, while Lee would add 14. The Hoosiers would host their next three contests against Ohio University, Kansas State, and Detroit. Big Walt Bellamy would provide the scoring for the Hoosiers with 24 against Ohio, 23 against Kansas State, and 35 against Detroit, as the Hoosiers of McCracken reeled off three straight wins. The Detroit game was worthy of note in that Bellamy's 35 would outscore All-American and later NBA All-Star Dave DeBusschere by a 35-to-28 margin.

Next, Mac's Hoosiers traveled to Indianapolis to take on Tony Hinkle's Butler Bulldogs and, behind Ballamy's 24, Radovich's 21, Bass' 16, and Lee's 13, captured their fourth contest in a row. Now they would face Notre Dame for the championship of the Hoosier Classic. Indiana would place four men in double figures as in front of 11,000 people they defeated Notre Dame, 71 to 60, for the mythical Hoosier Classic crown since the Hoosier Classic would not be an official tournament and no actual champion would exist over the years of this tourney between, Indiana, Butler, Notre Dame, and Purdue.

Indiana would travel 100 miles south to Louisville, Kentucky, to play in the second tournament of the season in the Bluegrass Festival. Indiana's first opponent was Maryland, whom they handled easily, 72 to 63, after leading at the half, 41 to 28. Then Indiana would take on the host, Peck Hickman's Louisville Cardinals. Both McCracken and Hickman were veteran coaches by now of national acclaim. McCracken's Hoosiers would come out on top, capturing the Bluegrass Crown, 90 to 71. Bellamy would lead the way with 24, but far from being a one-man show, he would have tremendous help from Wilkinson and Bass with 17 each, and Radovich would have 14.

Indiana would open the Big Ten season at home against Purdue. The Hoosiers were 8 and 1 and heavy favorites against their in-state rivals.

Purdue's All-American, Terry Dischinger, was not even expected to play because of illness. However, as is par for the course in the Big Ten, expect the unexpected. Dischinger would not only play, but score 30 points and lead the Boilers to a 79-76 win. In the process, Purdue would hold Bellamy to a season-low 8 points. Indiana would travel to Northwestern still reeling from the loss to Purdue. The Wildcats of Northwestern sprang yet another surprise on Indiana, coming from behind at half to defeat the Hoosiers, 61 to 57. Now Indiana had gone from 8 and 1 with the second-best preconference record (as compared to Ohio State's 9 and 0) to 8 and 3 with a conference record of 0 and 2—last in the Big Ten.

The Hoosiers traveled to Columbus to take on the Ohio State Buckeyes, who at 11 and 0 were first in the nation and conference. Indiana came out playing with the intensity that would make McCracken very proud, but the Hoosiers could not sustain their effort and would lose on this day to the Buckeyes by the slimmest of margins, 96 to 95. Indiana had now lost three straight games, all coming in conference play. A team that had looked like a challenger to the Buckeyes for the conference crown was looking up from the very bottom of the league.

To McCracken's and his players' credit, they did not roll over and give up. No, in fact they would do just the opposite, starting with their very next game. Indiana would next play the Wolverines of Michigan and start a winning streak by beating Michigan, 77 to 72. Indiana would travel out of conference, going to Chicago and playing DePaul of Chicago. Bellamy came up big in the contest with 34, and Indiana handed the host Blue Demons an 82-to-76 defeat.

Indiana would return to Big Ten action in Bloomington against Northwestern. The Hoosiers would capture their second straight Big Ten win, 76 to 58, over the Wildcats. Indiana was now riding a three-game winning streak and ready to take on the Badgers of Wisconsin at Madison with a chance to even their conference record. Walt Bellamy would be a beast on the boards, with 16 rebounds to go with his 32 points, and Indiana turned away the Badgers by 12, 97 to 85.

Indiana would begin a three-game home stand against Iowa, Wisconsin, and Michigan. Indiana captured all the contests behind the balanced scoring of the starters for Branch. Indiana under Branch was now 6 and 3 in the Big Ten and in second place behind undefeated Ohio State.

Indiana hit the road again, this time going first to Iowa and then to Illinois. At Iowa, Radovich would lead the way with 21 points and Indiana would win, 79 to 64. Indiana would then go to Illinois, and Big Walt would go off for 42 points as the Hoosiers conquered Illinois, 92 to 78.

There were now just three games remaining in the season. Indiana would defeat Minnesota, 78 to 74, to set up a payback game against the Ohio State Buckeyes. The Hoosiers would be without the services of starting guard Herb Lee, and yet Indiana would play inspired basketball. Ohio State All-Americans Jerry Lucas and John Havlicek would score 27 and 25 points, respectively, but the day and this game would belong to the Hoosiers. Indiana placed all five starters in double figures, led by Walt Bellamy's 24, Wilkerson's 21, Long's 19, and 13 each from Radovich and Hall. Indiana would crush the Buckeyes, 99 to 83, playing the very last game played in the Old Fieldhouse on Seventh Street. Branch had christened the Old Fieldhouse with its first points; now he would say farewell with one of his greatest coaching efforts.

Indiana rounded out the season on the road with a win over Michigan State, 86 to 80. Indiana would end the season as the hottest team in the country on a 12-game win streak, including a 16-point victory over the eventual national champions, the Ohio State Buckeyes. The Hoosiers would finish second in the Big Ten with a record of 11 and 3, including winning their last 11 in a row. They would finish the season as McCracken's third team to win 20 or more games in a season (the other two being both the '40 and '53 national championship teams). They would finish the season ranked seventh in the nation; remember, only the champion of the conference could play in the NCAAs at this time. They would be the champions of both the Indiana Classic and the Blue Grass Festival Tournament. Walt Bellamy would be named to the All-American team and join the 1960 Olympic team, considered by many to be the best amateur team put together.

It can be argued, and I would make the argument, that if the NCAA tourney were as it is today, then indeed McCracken would have had his third national championship title. Pete DiPrimo and Rick Notter would say in their book, *Hoosier Handbook*, that McCracken addressed a group of people at Indiana's annual awards banquet by saying, "This bunch of boys could beat anyone in the country. I'd love to walk out of here and play in the NCAA. It's probably my fault we lost those three games. I had the boys too high for some of the non-conference games. Sometimes it does you good to lose a game or two early in the season. ... Too much publicity, we won the tournaments at Indianapolis and Louisville and we were getting all those write ups. The players came home with gold watches and they didn't come down to earth until they lost."[2]

Still, all in all, McCracken and his Hoosiers had one of the finest seasons in Indiana basketball history.

# Chapter 18

## THE BELLAMY, RAYL, AND BOLYARD YEARS

T HE SIXTIES HAD STARTED OUT SO PROMISING FOR McCRACKEN AND
the Hoosiers. There was the 12-game winning streak to end the 1960
season, a streak that had started at Michigan on January 11, 1960. The
Hoosiers would race off to a 6 and 3 record to begin the 1960–61 season.
The sixties, however, would bring heartache as well as success to both
McCracken and Indiana.

In April of 1960, the NCAA would announce they had found major rule violations against the Indiana football program and its coach Phil Dickens. Years later, Dr. Robert Milisin would share that the actions of Coach Dickens did not differ a lot from those of Ohio State, Michigan, and Purdue. When Dickens pled his case with President Wells, the latter responded by insisting that Indiana University would always choose the straight and narrow path.

The NCAA threw the book at the Hoosiers and disallowed any Indiana team from any sport participating in any postseason tournament play. These sanctions would hit Indiana's two most successful programs, basketball and swimming, hardest. The penalty, which would be in effect for four years, was appealed by both Indiana and the Big Ten Conference because of its harshness. The penalty would stand, however, and make it very difficult for Coach McCracken to recruit; in fact, Dick Sparks of Bloomington would be the only recruit for the 1960 class.

Unfortunately for Branch, that would not be the only obstacle. Branch would also be faced with the dilemma of the Orwig hiring. In 1961, Indiana hired a new athletic director in Bill Orwig. McCracken until this time had always gotten along with his athletic directors, but this time would be different. Orwig did not take a liking to Branch. No one knows for sure why, but many of Branch's friends and family felt Orwig was afraid that Branch wanted to be the athletic director, which they said was a job that Branch in fact did not want. The animosity would get so bad that Orwig would accuse Branch of recruiting violations to the point of asking him to take a lie detector test.

Bobby Leonard would comment about the situation in a 1989 interview, saying, "There was a recruiting situation, and he had Branch take a lie detector test, which was totally ridiculous."[1] Branch's son Dave would say of the situation, "He should never have done it, but he did. So he took the test and of course it proved he had not lied. I think it hurt him more than anything else that happened at Indiana University, more than any critism, was the fact that Indiana University doubted what he had said."[2] Branch, in true champion's fashion, would weather both storms; however hurt he was, he would always love his university, for IU was in his blood and he was always in IU's and her fans.

The basketball part of the 1961 season would begin with the return of All-American Walt Bellamy for his senior season, along with forward Charlie Hall and guards Gary Long and Jerry Bass. Indiana would bring up to the varsity (remember, freshmen were not allowed to play varsity level at this time) Tom Bolyard, Jimmy Rayl, and Ray Pavy. Pavy and Rayl had taken part in what many consider to be one of the most classic Indiana high school shootouts of all time. Rayl would represent Kohomo High School and Pavy, New Castle. Rayl would pour in 49 and Pavy 51—oh my, what a shootout! McCracken would smile with delight at the prospect of both joining the Hoosiers.

Pavy would say of the three sophomores, "We had different talents. Tom was very athletic—he could really jump and run. Jim could really shoot—when he crossed the half court line, he was in range. I was more of a driver, a stop and shoot player."[3] Bolyard would say of Pavy, "He was really a big guard. He could post up."[4]

The 1960–61 season was played at what would be called the "New Fieldhouse." The New Fieldhouse would be a tempory home for the Hoosiers until the building of Assembly Hall some 11 years later—far longer than Indiana had expected. (Writer's Note: As one who had the wonderful opportunity to watch games there from the beginning, it was indeed a wonderful place to watch a game. From the sawdust floors, to the raised court, to the closeness of the fans to the action, it was a fun place to watch the hurryin' Hoosiers.

Indiana would start the season at home on Saturday, December 3, against Indiana State. Indiana would win before a crowd of 9,236 fans. Bellamy would begin his senior season with a 20-point game. Tom Bolyard scored 14, while Rayl added 12. Indiana would lead by 15 at the half, 37 to 22, and walk away victorious, 80 to 53.

Indiana would go on the road and defeat Kansas State, 98 to 80, in game two of the season. Pavy would remember that game for a different reason: "We were one of the first college teams to fly, and we would use a Purdue pilot because Purdue had an aeronautics school. Well, a storm comes up and we get lost and land a couple hours from Manhattan, Kansas. We had to bus to Kansas State, and of course you can imange how mad Branch was and of course it was a Purdue pilot on top of everything else, which just made matters that much worse."[5] Bellamy would lead the way in scoring at Kansas State with 26 points while Bolyard, Long, and Bass would contribute 22, 17, and 13, respectively.

Indiana went next go to Detroit, and Pavy would remember, "As a rookie finding out about Mac's culinary desires, we were told when you go to Detroit that you went to a certain restaurant, and Branch would order everyone marinated herring. We were all told that Branch expected us all to eat his favorite dish, so marinated herring it was."[6]

Indiana would lose to Detroit in a heartbreaker, 81 to 79, on a last-second shot in double overtime. This would be the second clash for future NBA stars Dave DeBusschere and Walt Bellamy. This time, DeBusschere would outscore Bell 23 to 17 to best the Big Bell. Indiana would return to Bloomington and defeat both Missouri and Nevada by scores of 66 to 55 and 80 to 52. Indiana would go back on the road and, behind Bellamy's 29, beat the Irish, 74 to 69.

Bellamy was showing signs of becoming an excellent pro candidate, and he would be interviewed about his progress in his senior year and what type of pro player he might become. Bellamy would say, "Whether I do well or not, I owe an awful lot to Coach McCracken. He encouraged me to work hard. I skipped rope, shot 100 free throws every night after practice, and worked on my shooting and rebounding."[7] Pavy would tell of the day in practice when Branch took matters in his own hands. "One day, Walt wasn't working as hard as Branch wanted him to, so Branch would rip off his sweatshirt—Branch's practice outfit was a gray sweatshirt, T-shirt, gray pants, and tennis shoes—and went into the post against Bell. Even though Branch was around 50, he would take on our All-American center, Bellamy, and whip him up and down. He just took him to school. We all wondered what kind of player Branch must have been in his day."[8]

*Walt Bellamy rebounds as Gordon Mickey (30), Tom Bolyard (45), Jerry Bass (15), and Ernie Wilhoit (32) look on, December 12, 1960.*

The Hoosiers' win at Fort Wayne over Notre Dame would be a very special victory for McCracken as it gave him 300 wins at Indiana. Indiana would travel out west to participate in the Los Angeles Classic just before the New Year. On the way out, Branch made sure the players were wearing their coats and ties, much to the players' disappointment. The players knew that Ohio State had made the same trip the year before in their T-shirts so they were able to get better tans. Upperclassmen Bellamy, Long, and Hall would lead Indiana to a 58-to-50 victory over Stanford with 20, 10 and 10 points, respectively.

Game two in LA would pit two old friends against each other. UCLA's Wooden would get the best of McCracken on this night, 94 to 72. Indiana closed out their part of the tournament, losing to Southern Cal, 90 to 71, despite Bellamy's 27. The trip to LA wasn't complete for the team, however, as McCracken took the Hoosiers to Disneyland for the day for a little fun. You could say it was Magic Kingdom meets "Magic Basketball Kingdom," McCracken-style.

McCracken would take his Hoosiers to Michigan to begin the '61 Big Ten season. Behind Bellamy's 23 and Long's 18, the Hoosiers won, 81 to 70. Indiana returned home to take on the Michigan State Spartans. Indiana would win, 79 to 55, to push their mark in the Big Ten to 2 and 0.

Indiana would not play for the next 19 days because of semester finals and break, but when they returned to action, they took on DePaul of Chicago. McCracken always wanted to start the schedule after semester break with a nonconference team. Indiana would defeat DePaul by 3, 81 to 78, as the three Bs led the way. Bellamy would have 25, followed by Bass's 23 and Bolyard's 12; Rayl would also throw in 12 for the Hoosiers. Indiana would lose their first Big Ten game, 66 to 58, to Minnesota, before besting Northwestern in Bloomington, 90 to 78, behind Bellamy's 34.

Indiana went on a three-game losing streak, falling to Ohio State, Iowa, and Purdue. Ohio State had been waiting for the Hoosiers after losing to Indiana the year before in Bloomington and hearing people say that Indiana had a better team. It had been on February 2, during Bellamy's sophomore year, that Indiana had come to Columbus and set a single-game Big Ten scoring record in defeating Ohio State, 122 to 92. Ohio State was ready for revenge; Bellamy's last trip to Columbus would not be pretty. The game was a clash between two coaching giants in the Big Ten, and Ohio State would clearly outclass Indiana that day. The game would turn out to be a one-sided affair. In the last few minutes of the game, Hall of Famer John Havlicek would hit a shot to give Ohio State 100 points in the game; it was not until that moment that Ohio State head coach Taylor took out his starters. The score read 100 to 65 in Ohio

State's favor. Coach McCracken stormed off the court without shaking Coach Taylor's hand, as he was upset with Taylor for running up the score.

*Rayl scores a jumper over Ohio State as Branch's future successor, Bob Knight (24), looks on, February 20, 1961.*

Pavy would recall in this game that "the Ohio State football players would seat at one end of the court, and during the course of the game, a loose ball would go in that direction. I would go after the ball, and Havlicek would push me into the football players that would begin to beat me up. I got out of the mess and as Havlicek and I were running down the court, he said to me, 'Welcome to the league, rookie.'"[9] Indiana would finally end its three-game skid by beating Wisconsin on the road, 98 to 84, with the help of 12 field goals each from both Bolyard and Bellamy.

Number 1 Ohio State would come to Bloomington and win by four. The Hoosiers would host Illinois on February 25, and Walt Bellamy scored 22 points and hauled in 18 rebounds as the Hoosiers gave Branch his 400th career coaching victory, 93 to 82.

Indiana finished out the season on a three-game winning streak defeating Iowa, Wisconsin, and Michigan. On March 11, in Bloomington, All-American Walt Bellamy would send home both the Hoosier faithful and Coach McCracken wishing he would have one more year. Bellamy hit 10 field goals and 8 free throws for a total of 28 points, but it was what Walt did on the boards that was totally amazing. Walt set a Big Ten record that still stands, with 33 rebounds in the game. Pavy would say, "We kidded Walt after the game, telling Walt, 'We missed all those shots tonight so you could get all those rebounds."[10]

McCracken would say at the start of the season that Bellamy "has improved more in three years than anyone I've ever had. This should be his greatest year ever."[11] For the year, Bellamy would average 21.8 points a game and haul in 17.8 rebounds a game, an Indiana record. Indiana would go 15 and 9, finishing 8 and 6 for fourth place in the Big Ten. Bellamy would again be an All-American.

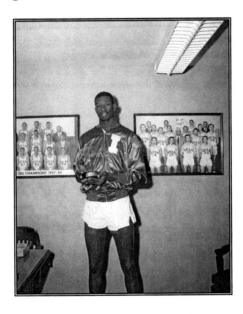

*Walt Bellamy, McCracken's first Olympian*

The 1962–63 Season would feature Rayl and Bolyard. With the loss of Big Bell, Indiana's string of All-American centers would come to an end under McCracken. Starting with Garrett, Schlundt, Dees, and Bellamy,

McCracken had been blessed with tremendous talent in the post position; however, the '61–62 season would leave McCracken without a star in the post. McCracken would state that because of the abundant wealth of talent at center, Indiana had strayed somewhat from the running game that Branch had made famous. Now, as the '61–62 season approached, his desire was to run again. "Now we intend to go back to it and be a running club. We've played the other fellow's game long enough," McCracken said in the '61–62 media guide.[12] Branch would express his interest in seeing just what kind of team Indiana would be. He was sure of his team's speed, shooting ability, and deftness in handling the ball.

Indiana would open on the road for the first time in 17 seasons at Des Moines, Iowa. Drake led the Hoosiers by 17 at the half. 53 to 36. Indiana would battle back in the second half using a full court press. However, the deficit was too much to overcome, and Indiana would lose its season opening, 90 to 81.

The Hoosiers would come home to face New Mexico State. Although Indiana trailed at the half, 34 to 29, behind Rayl's 21 second-half points, Indiana would rally to win, 74 to 68, and Rayl would account for 34. Number 4, Kansas State, came to Bloomington and rode out of town with an 88-to-78 victory. Rayl would put up 23 points, while Bolyard would add 19. Indiana would travel to Greensboro, North Carolina, and even their record at 2 and 2, defeating the Tar Heels, 78 to 70, as two legends in coaching passed like ships in the night: McCracken in the twilight of his career and Dean Smith at the beginning of his.

Next up for Indiana was hosting Detroit. Despite DeBusschere's 29, Indiana staged a 92-to-84 victory. Rayl would match DeBusschere's 29 with 29 of his own, and Bolyard would chip in 21, with Bass adding 14. Bolyard and Rayl would combine for 56 against Arizona State, Bolyard with 31 of them, as Indiana won to give Mac's Men a record of 4 and 2. Indiana would go on the road and lose to both Iowa State and Loyola of Chicago before heading to Fort Wayne to play the Irish of Notre Dame.

On January 2 of 1962, the Hoosiers would celebrate the dawning of a new year as they tied their own Big Ten record with a 122-to-95 victory. Before the game, McCracken had decided to start sophomore center Dick Sparks in the middle. Sparks rewarded McCracken with a 16-point, 15-rebound performance. Sparks would say of the opportunity to start at Fort Wayne against Notre Dame, "We were players short at the center position. There was Dave Granger, Winston Fairfield, and myself. We were all competing against each other in practice. I was more aggressive in fundamentals such as blocking out, defense, and rebounding. In practice, Branch had everyone practice against each other for playing time in our 2-on-2s. Charlie Hall and I had hook shots, which helped offensively. Coach McCracken gave me the nod for the start against Notre Dame. The Fort Wayne Coliseum was a real nice place to play, very modern. We all played well that day. Branch's offense was very simple—at the end of three passes, you had better be shooting the ball."[13] Sparks would be McCracken's only recruit for that class because of the NCAA sanctions. Sparks would relay that he had over 100 scholarship offers coming out of Bloomington High School, but he had narrowed his choice down to 5 schools: Houston, Kansas State, Arizona State, Butler, and IU. He finally chose IU because of the iconic McCracken and IU's location playing at home. And of course when you score 122 points, no one man is going to account for all of them; besides Sparks's 16, Rayl would have 28, Hall 22, and Bass 21.

McCracken's often-used phrase of "run, run, run," was fully in effect. Rayl would lead five players in double figures as Indiana defeated Michigan State to start the Big Ten season. Then Rayl would go on a run of three games like no Hoosier before or since. First, Indiana traveled to Minnesota and the Hoosiers lost a close encounter, 104–100. Rayl would light up the Gophers for 32. Next, Indiana went to Chicago to play DePaul. Rayl would hit 16 field goals and 9 free throws for 41 points as Indiana defeated the Blue Demons, 98–89. The third game was played in Bloomington against Minnesota. Rayl would set a new Indiana and Big Ten record for points in a game. With just a few seconds left in overtime, Rayl hit a 20-foot jump shot to give Indiana a 105-to-104 win. Connecting on 20 of 29 field goals and 16 of 20 free throws, Rayl would finish the game with 56 points. McCracken would call it "one of the greatest exhibitions of outside shooting that I have even seen."[14] Rayl would say years later, "I had some pretty good games my junior and senior years, but there again it was because Branch let me do some crazy things on the floor that a lot of coaches would take you out of the game for. You shoot a lot of shots, you're going to look bad once in a while. I might miss six or seven shots in a row, but Branch would never take me out."[15] In that three-game stretch, Rayl scored 129 points for a 43-point average, without the benefit of a 3-point shot.

Indiana would next go to Northwestern. The Wildcats would "hold" Rayl to 24, but the Hoosiers prevailed, 72 to 71. Indiana would travel to Illinois and lose, 96 to 85. The Hoosiers' losing streak would be extended to two with a home loss to the Badgers, 105 to 94. Rayl would hit for 44. Indiana would lose to Purdue, 105 to 93, but beat Iowa and Michigan behind Rayl's 35 and 34 points. Indiana traveled to the state of Michigan and come home with two losses, despite Rayl scoring 31 and 37 points.

Finally, Indiana would come home to face Purdue and Illinois. Much to Branch's pleasure, Mac's Men defeated rival Purdue, 88 to 71, behind Rayl's 37 and Bolyard's 21. The Purdue game would be marred by a fight between the Boilers' Darrell McQuitty and Indiana's Gordon Mickey. The Hoosiers would run past Illinois, 104 to 92, behind Rayl's 37 and Bolyard's 22. Indiana would close the season in disappointing fashion, losing to the Buckeyes, 90 to 65. McCracken had promised a running team, and the '62 Hoosiers were just that, scoring 100 or more points four times and averaging more than 87 points a game, which was a new Indiana school record. However, Indiana would give up an average of 88 points a game. The Hoosiers finished the season 13 and 11, and 7 and 7 in the Big Ten for a fourth-place finish. Hotshot Jimmy Rayl would be named an All-American.

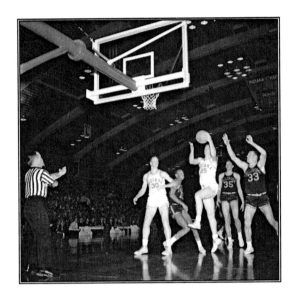

*Tom Van Arsdale scores a layup over Illinois as brother Dick watches.*

*McCracken's big four of 1963 get in on the action (L–R, Dick Van Arsdale, Tom Van Arsdale, Tom Bolyard, and Jimmy Rayl).*

The 1962–63 season would see a return of IU's two leading scorers, Jimmy Rayl and Tom Bolyard. Prize recruits Tom and Dick Van Arsdale and Jon McGlocklin were now sophomores and able to make their debut to the varsity scene. McCracken would say over and over again that "convincing them to come to Indiana was my greatest recruiting achievement." Given the context of the situation between the Vans' ability and the NCAA probation, this statement could very well be true. Rayl's 29.8 average and Bolyard's 18.6 average were keys for the coming season.

Indiana would start the season on December the first in Bloomington hosting Virginia. Rayl would start his senior year as he had left off his junior year with 35 points. The Vans' college debut would be impressive, with 20 combined points; Dick would have 11 and Tom 9. The Hoosiers of the '63 Season lacked proven height but they did have outstanding speed. Their tallest, Winston Fairfield (alias Winnie the Pooh), would stand at six-foot-ten but would play in only six games, averaging 1.8 points a contest. Branch would mainly rely on seven players, and the Vans and McGlocklin would stand the tallest at six-foot-five. Bolyard, the team captain, would check in at six-foot-four, while Rayl and Redenbaugh would be measured at six-two and little Al Harden would be listed at five-foot-ten.

*Rayl scores a jumper over Drake.*

After an opening season win and being ranked number 8 in the nation, Indiana would lose their next two games at home against Drake and Iowa State. They would travel to Missouri and lose a heartbreaker, 52 to 51. Missouri would lead Indiana at the half, 31 to 20. Rayl would lead the way in a very low scoring affair with 13, followed by Bolyard's 10 and Dick Van Arsdale's 11. Bolyard would share how hard McCracken would take a defeat: "We got beat at Missouri and we should have won that game. It was an old Fieldhouse at Missouri, and after the game, we got out of the shower and couldn't find the coach. He was walking around the dirt track and he asked me to walk with him. We walked a couple of laps and he just picked my brain as to what we could do to help the team. We just walked that track. He took a loss hard now, I tell you, he took it really hard."[16]

Indiana came home to host an undefeated North Carolina team. Indiana would receive balanced scoring, as four starters reached double figures. McCracken had pushed all the right buttons by starting Franklin's Jon McGlocklin for the first time in his career. Moose would go for 20 points to go along with Rayl's 24, Bolyard's 18, and Tom Van Arsdale's 16 as Indiana would win, 90 to 76. Indiana would go to Detroit and make it two in a row. The entire starting lineup would score in double figures, with Rayl topping them all with 32.

Indiana would host undefeated and future NCAA champs Loyola of Chicago; the Hoosiers would lose in a shootout, 106 to 94. Tom Bolyard would lead the way with 2, followed closely by Rayl's 26. Indiana dropped the next two contests on the road, 88 to72 vs. Kansas State, and then they would suffer a heartbreaking loss to Notre Dame at Fort Wayne, 73 to 70. The loss at Fort Wayne was so difficult because the Hoosiers led at halftime, 46 to 30. Indiana was now 3 and 6 and reeling.

Branch gathered the troops and Indiana began the Big Ten portion of the season with a 96-to-84 win over Michigan State at East Lansing. Jimmy Rayl would connect on 16 jumpers and 12 free throws to total 44 points against the Spartans. Bolyard would chip in 25 points, while Dick VanArsdale would add 15. Next up in Bloomington, much to Branch's delight, Indiana would send Purdue back to West Lafayette 85-to-71 losers behind Rayl's 25. Indiana would run the streak to four with wins over DePaul and Purdue.

In the DePaul game at home, the Hoosiers were down at the half by 15, 43 to 28. Hall of Fame Coach Ray Meyer of DePaul would say, "It so happened that we were ahead at halftime and Indiana had a great basketball team, and Branch was bawling them out and the walls were thin in the locker room, and we were on the other side so we could hear everything Branch said, so I just listened and let him give our team their pep talk."[17] A fired-up Indiana team came out in the second half and defeated DePaul by 1, 76 to 75, on a tip-in shot from Paoli's own Steve Redenbaugh.

Indiana was then shocked at home by Northwestern by a score of 100 to 87. Tom Bolyard would say that after the game "that even though I led the team with 28 points, Mac would rip into me and only me for what seemed like 20 minutes. I went back to the house and got a call from Branch and he began by saying that he had looked at the scorebook, and at that point I just hung up the phone. The next day in practice, Branch called me over and said he just did that to set an example for the younger players." Tom wasn't convinced, but it should be noted that Tom would always maintain that Branch was like a second father to him. Tom would say that one game really did cost Indiana the Big Ten Championship: "We really should have won that game."[18]

Indiana would travel to take on number 4 Illinois at Champaign. The two teams would put on a scoring clinic, with Indiana coming out on the short, 104 to 101. Rayl and Bolyard led the Hoosiers in scoring, with Bolyard putting in 35 and Rayl 31. Indiana then dropped its third in a row to Michigan by 4.

The Hoosiers came home to Bloomington, and this would prove to be a cure for McCracken's men as his team beat Minnesota by 12 behind Rayl's 32, Dick Van's 20, Bolyard's 17, and Tom Van's 14. Then, on February 16, Indiana would have a return engagement with Illinois at Bloomington. Indiana trailed at the half by 9, 50 to 41. The Hoosiers would rally in the second half to score 62 points and win, 103 to 100. Tom Bolyard would lead the way with 34, and Rayl would add 29. The Van Arsdale twins would contribute 12 and 11 points.

Indiana would travel to Iowa and escape with a 1-point victory, 72 to 71. The biggest note of the game would not be who scored for the Hoosiers, but rather who the Hawkeyes shut down. Iowa would hold All-American

Jimmy Rayl to just 1 field goal for 2 points. Branch knew, however, that it would just mean pain for some other team, and no one had to wait long. Indiana's next game was an afternoon affair in Bloomington against Michigan State. The game was played the day after the twins' birthday, but the day would belong to one man. February 23, 1963, would be the day that Rayl would explode. Jimmy Rayl took a record 48 shots; he would connect on 23 of them, adding 10 free throws for a total of 56 points—a new record for a game played in regulation. Rayl had scored 56 in overtime against Minnesota the year before. McCracken would take Rayl out with three minutes to go, and Rayl would recall what happened next: "As I left the game and was walking across the line to the bench, all I could hear was booing and I couldn't understand it—I thought I had a pretty good game. Then I realized they were booing Mac for taking me out." Rayl would relate that on that day by today's standards, he could have scored 80 points. He would say that 17 of those 23 baskets were from 3-point range and at that time the clock didn't stop the way it does today; plus with the three minutes he left early in the game, he would have had 8 more minutes of play. Jim said, "I know I could have scored 7 more points with 8 more minutes."[19] The 56 points, combined with the 44 against State at State, would give Rayl a total of 100 points in two games that season against Michigan State.

Indiana would lose their next two games to Wisconsin and Minnesota on the road. The Hoosiers would finish the 1962–63 Season at home. On March 4, they defeated Michigan, 104 to 96, as Bolyard led the way with 31, followed by Tom Van Arsdale's 26, Rayl's 23, and Dick Van Arsdale's 15. The final game of the season would see Ohio State visit Bloomington to take on Indiana. An Ohio State win, and the Buckeyes would win the Big Ten title and a trip to the NCAA tournament; however, an Indiana win would give Illinois a tie for the title and send Illinois to the tourney and the Buckeyes home. The game would feature the top three scorers in the league with Ohio State's Gary Bradds number one, followed by Indiana's Rayl and Bolyard at two and three. It would be a close affair the entire game, with Ohio State in front by 2 at the half, 36 to 34.

Rayl would talk about the game, saying, "Bradds started talking and complaining about something, and I did something I really did not do. I yelled back at him to 'stop complaining, you big crybaby.' Bradds didn't like me saying that, so he swung at me. Luckily, he missed. He was really big—if he had hit me, it would have hurt."[20] Bolyard and Dick Van stepped in and order was restored. Rayl would recall in the overtime session, "Jerry Bass threw the ball into me and as I turned to go up court, I got hit. There were 9 seconds left and we were up by 1. I went down on the floor and our fans came on the court. I was told there were about 150 fans out there. I was really hurt, but I went to the line to shoot my free throws. I took my first shot and the ball went underneath the basket. I shot the second free throw a lot harder and it went in."[21] Indiana would win by 2, 87 to 85, and the fans would rush the floor for a second time, this time in celebration. Rayl would relate that he had a separated collarbone and if there had been any more games, he could not have played.

Indiana would finish 13 and 11 for the season for the second straight year. Branch's team would finish third in the Big Ten behind co-leaders Ohio State and Illinois. Bolyard would say to this day that if "we hadn't lost to Northwestern, we would have won it all that year."[22] Rayl would be named All-American and he and Bolyard would be named All-Big Ten First Team.

*Picture of Jimmy Rayl with Branch (Courtesy Jimmy Rayl)*

# Chapter 19

## BRANCH: THE LAST YEARS

THE YEAR WAS 1963. INDIANA HAD FINISHED THE PREVIOUS YEAR 13 and 11, 7 and 7 in the Big Ten to finish in the upper division of the conference in fourth place. The Hoosiers had lost, however, the conference's number two and three leading scorers in Jimmy Rayl and Tom Bolyard. Branch would bring back into the fold for their junior years the Van Arsdales, Tom and Dick, Jon McGlocklin, Steve Redenbaugh, and Al Harden. He would add junior college transfer Larry Cooper, from Hutchinson, Kansas, and sophomores Max Walker from Milwaukee, Wisconsin, and Gary Grieger from Evansville.

Walker would recall his recruitment to Indiana: "Indiana had an outstanding physical education department, one of the best in the nation, and everyone knew about Branch and Indiana basketball. I had received letters from almost every Big Ten school, but I had decided I wanted to go to IU, so I wrote Indiana a letter expressing my desire to come there. The other thing about Indiana that was perfect was that it was far enough from home, Milwaukee, Wisconsin, that I won't run home all the time, but close enough I could get home if I needed to."

McCracken would address the players and strengths of the team as he saw them in the 1963–64 media guide. McCracken on McGlocklin: "Jon is far too good a basketball player to sit on the bench. When he's in the middle, he really makes them go. He'll play some in the pivot regardless of how well Peyser or Cooper does. There will be situations where he'll be better suited than the others. And when he isn't in the pivot, you probably will see him at forward or at guard. He can do a fine job at any of them." Branch would turn his attention to the Van Arsdales: "They're two of the finest we've ever had. Last year they had all the pressure in the world on them, but they came through like champions. This year I'll be greatly surprised if they're not greater yet. They're smart and they were learning all the time last year. That experience will show. Both are hitting much better from outside and their ability to connect from outside should make their driving game more effective." McCracken would say of the Hoosiers' speed, "This is one of our strong points. With McGlocklin in the pivot, we're as fast as last year. We're going to run. We've had success with it and that's where the squad is strong." Mac would say, "We can shoot. Last year's was the second best shooting team on average that we've ever had and we should be just as good. Our defense must improve but our team spirit is good. They think they're going to win the conference and I wouldn't have them think differently. They're hustlers and they'll battle."[1]

McCracken would start his twenty-third year coaching at IU on November 30 as the Hoosiers opened their season at home against Southern Illinois. Branch would start junior college transfer Larry Cooper at center, and Cooper would respond with 24 points and 17 rebounds in an 80-to-65 Indiana victory. Cooper would say, "After the game, which was my first game at IU, I had such a good game against Southern Illinois that I walked out and my parents and girlfriend were there and I just said, 'Well here we are in the big time.' The next day in practice Coach McCracken looked at me and said, 'They're not all going to be that easy. You may have had a good game, but they're not all going to be that good. Next week we play Notre Dame—they've got this big clown that's going to sit on you.'"[2]

Indiana on December 4 would go to the Fort Wayne Coliseum to take on the fighting Irish of Notre Dame. The Hoosiers fell behind at half-time by 7, 47 to 40; however, Indiana would rally by scoring 68 points in the second half to win, 108 to 102. It would be the Van Arsdale show in the second half as Dick Van Arsdale scored 25 points and brother Tom hit for 20 ooints. For the game, the twins each connected on 15 baskets from the field, while Dick hit 12 free throws and Tom had 4 free throws. Dick Van Arsdale would have his career-high game at 42 points, while Tom would also hit for a career-high at 34 points, keeping their careers eerily identical. Cooper would laugh and say, tongue-in-cheek, years later, "Branch was right, they weren't all as easy as my first game, but really I think Notre Dame was concentrating so hard on me it allowed Tom and Dick to get free for all those points." Cooper would add, "Really, they were something else that night."[3] Indiana would next play their second straight game on a neutral court, this time in Charlotte, North Carolina. They played the Tar Heels of North Carolina and despite Dick's 24 and Tom's 17, IU would suffer their first defeat of the season, 77 to 70. Indiana would drop their second in a row to Kansas State, 93 to 84.

Indiana, at 2 and 2, hosted Missouri, and the Hoosiers did not show any Hoosier hospitality, winning 100 to 76. Tom and Dick Van Arsdale were men among boys that night as Tom scored 26 while Dick added 25. Dick would have a career-high 26 rebounds while Tom would collect 17 boards. Cooper and Redenbaugh would chip in 16 points apiece while McGlocklin had 12. Two days later, Indiana would hit the century mark for their second straight game as they topped Detroit, 110 to 92. Dick would have 28 while Tom hit for 25, McGlocklin added 22, and Cooper, Redenbaugh and Grieger would have 8, followed by Walkers's 4.

Indiana at this point was 4 and 2 and feeling very good, however, the season was about to start to spiral downward. The Hoosiers were about to start an eight-game losing streak. The streak started on December 20 at Corvallis, Oregon, as Indiana lost to Oregon State, 70 to 57. The next day in Portland, Oregon, Indiana lost again to Oregon State, this time 56 to 52. The Hoosiers would travel to Chicago, and despite Dick Van Arsdale's 36 points, would lose to Loyola, 105 to 92. The losing continued with Iowa, 72 to 71; Northwestern, 79 to 65; Michigan State, 107 to 103; DePaul, 85 to 78; and Purdue, 87 to 84.

The Hoosiers would finally break into the winning column again with an exciting 104-to-96 win over Illinois. The game, played before 8,000 Hoosier fans, would see Tom Van Arsdale and Jon McGlocklin score 27 points apiece, while Dick would add 25. Tom would add 13 rebounds, while Jon had 11 and Dick would contribute 15 to the effort. Because of the eight-game losing streak, many fans were upset with McCracken, calling for his job. However, the Hoosier football team formed a wall along the entrance to the court to show their support for McCracken. Indiana's victory would quiet the so-called fans. Indiana would lose three more games and IU's record stood at 5 and 13.

*Dick Van Arsdale gathers in a rebound as Tom watches.*

McCracken wasn't done. The Hoosiers would finish winning four of their last six, starting with an exciting double overtime win at Madison. McGlocklin led the way with 22 while Tom and Dick each had 21. Dick's last two points were a tip-in to capture the Hoosier victory, 82 to 80. Indiana would crush Purdue, 92 to 79, behind Tom's 30, McGlocklin's 24, and Dick's 17. Indiana would then host Wisconsin and this time, it would not be a 2-point affair, as Indiana would roll over Wisconsin, 108 to 82. Dick led the way with 26, followed by Tom's 23, McGlocklin's 20, Redenbaugh's 13, and Cooper's 8. Indiana dropped the next two before finishing the season on a winning note, 76 to 68 over Northwestern. The Hoosiers would finish eighth in the Big Ten with a 5 and 9 record while finishing 9 and 15 overall, giving Branch only his third sub-500 season out of the 23 he had coached at IU.

Jack Schneider, seeing the stress the eight-game losing streak had on Branch, wrote an open letter to Branch saying, "I realize basketball has been practically your entire life, from your days as a star at Monrovia High School and Indiana and continuing through your distinguished 31-year coaching career. But is it worth all this anguish and torment? It can't be. You're 56 years old, Mac, with a lot of good living ahead of you, if your health holds out. I wonder how long it can if the strain you have experienced the last few weeks goes on much longer."[4] Branch would have one year to go, and what a year it would turn out to be.

McCracken would address the Hoosier's prospects in the Indiana Media Guide for the 1964–65 Season: "I think our strongest points are speed and shooting. We've got lots of speed and we've got good shooters." McCracken would go on to say, "In any event, I think we'll have a team which on a given night can beat a pretty good ball club. I'm confident we can rebound with most of them. To do well this year, we're going to have to win those close ones we were dropping last year. Those losses made us an also-ran instead of a contender. We've always been a second-half club, coming on stronger near the end. In fact, in the past

I've always felt pretty good when we stayed close during the first three-fourths of the game. But last season we led at half-time of most games and then faded off in the second. This is something we'll have to change. Defense is the toughest thing to teach in today's game, especially with a running ball club such as ours. A lot of people don't realize you sacrifice a lot of defense with a running game, but we feel our material is better suited to that kind of game, and I think that hoop is up there to shoot at. The ball control clubs are the ones with the defensive records, mainly because they hold the ball so much of the time. We have seed and we'll use it. Our running game may make us look bad on defense at times, but I'm sure our defense is going to be a lot better than it was."[5]

McCracken would see the defense improve from last year by his own hand. McCracken implemented a new 2-2-1 full-court press that Indiana would use after every made basket. McCracken would use his special weapon with this press, using the Van Arsdales as the ones up front of the 2-2-1. Just imagine bringing the ball up court and seeing two people trapping you who look like one. Branch realized this special gift of identical twins. He knew first-hand how hard it was to tell them apart. In fact, Tom would say, "Branch made Dick and me wear different-colored sweat socks during practice so that he could tell us apart." Tom would say how much Branch loved to tell that story.

Branch's last season would begin on December 1 against Ohio. Branch would suit up seven seniors for that first game in his last season. Those seniors were the Van Arsdales (Tom and Dick), Jon McGlocklin, Larry Cooper, Al Harden, Steve Redenbaugh, and Ron Peyser. Indiana would lead Ohio by 1 at the half, 37 to 36. The Hoosiers showed a balance in scoring that had been absent the year before. The Hoosiers were led by Dick Van's 22 points. Peyser would score 11, McGlocklin and Harden would contribute 10, while Tom Van had 9 and Cooper 7 as Indiana would win game one, 81 to 70.

Indiana next traveled to Manhattan to take on Kansas State. The Hoosiers trailed by 1 at the half, 33 to 34. The Hoosiers would score 41 second-half points while holding the wildcats to 36, led by Tom Van Arsdale's 26, Dick's 18, and McGlocklin's 16. Indiana would return home for game three against Oklahoma. The Hoosiers would jump out to a 15-point lead at half and go on to win, 87 to 69. McCracken would play 13 players, led by Dick Van Arsdale's 16 while subs Russell, Walker, and Inniger would score 6, 4, and 4, as Hoosier fans caught a glimpse into the future as all three players would play a huge roll in Indiana's success in the coming years for McCracken's hand-picked successor, Lou Watson.

Indiana's next game would be a Saturday afternoon affair. The Hoosiers would host the North Carolina Tar Heels and future NBA star, Billy Cunningham. The Hoosiers entertained the crowd of 10,000 by crushing the Tar Heels, 107 to 81. Branch's 2-2-1 full-court press was working to perfection and the seven seniors would score, from McGlocklin's 25 to Redenbaugh and Cooper's 8 points. Indiana would stay in Bloomington to face DePaul. The Hoosiers would lead the Blue Demons at half by 1 but outscored DePaul 49 to 37 in the second half to win, 91 to 78, behind McGlocklin's 24, Tom Van's 22, and Redenbaugh's 18.

Indiana would travel to Detroit and again take charge in the second half, outscoring Detroit 63 to 44 to capture their sixth straight win. Hoosier fortunes had indeed changed from a year ago: Instead of losing a lead in the second half, IU was playing McCracken ball and coming on strong in the second half. Tom Van Arsdale would lead five Hoosiers in double figures with 22 on the game. Indiana would next go to Fort Wayne for its annual battle with Notre Dame played before the IU faithful at the Fort Wayne Coliseum. Ten thousand fans would see Indiana's full-court press force the Irish into 23 turnovers as IU walked over Notre Dame, 107 to 81. Tom Van Arsdale again led Indiana in scoring with 21 points as five Hoosiers would strike for double figures. McCracken played all 13 players as Indiana went 7 and 0.

IU would travel to Memphis, Tennessee, for the Memphis State Invitational. The tourney was not televised, so Hoosier faithful gathered in their homes, some surrounding their Christmas tree, and tuned into their radios to hear the broadcast of the tourney. Indiana's first opponent was St. Louis. The Hoosiers buried St. Louis, 98 to 68, with four Hoosiers in double figures, led by McGlocklin's 29. Indiana would play the host, Memphis State, for the championship and again the Hoosiers' 2-2-1 press would help IU capture the title as Indiana beat Memphis State, 91 to 68. Tom Van Arsdale led the way with 21, followed by McGlocklin's 19, brother Dick's 15, and Redenbaugh's 10. Tom, Dick, and Jon McGlocklin would be named to the All-Tourney Team.

Indiana had now won nine straight games and would head into the Big Ten season ranked second in the nation behind Michigan. IU's first opponent was 6-ranked Illinois. Illinois jumped out to a 10-point halftime lead, but IU would fight back to lose a close one, 86 to 81. Illinois coach, Harry Combes, would say after the game that Indiana's press was the best in the nation and how thankful he was to not have to play IU at Bloomington.

IU would roar back to win three conference games in a row over Northwestern, at Iowa, and at Ohio State. The Iowa game would see three Hoosiers score 20 points or more: Redenbaugh would hit for 22, while McGlocklin and Dick Van each had 20. Indiana stood at 12 and 1, ranked fifth in the nation.

Indiana would come back to Bloomington to face an Iowa team they had beaten 7 days earlier by 9 at Iowa. However, the Hoosiers' backs would be against the wall. Star Jon McGlocklin was nursing an ankle injury and could not play, and in what some thought was a political move, the fire marshal had ruled that the New Fieldhouse did not have enough exits.

He would limit the amount of fans to 3,300 from the usual 10,000. Imagine the season ticket holders being told their tickets were no good—wow! Indiana would fall behind by 14 before mounting a charge and rallying to lose by 6 with a 74-to-68 final score.

*Tom and Dick Van Arsdale crash the boards for
Branch as Steve Redenbaugh looks on.*

Indiana would come back from semester break and hammer Loyola of Chicago 109–82. It would be the third game on the year in which the Hoosiers had scored 100 or more points. IU would play their sixth Big Ten game at home against Michigan State. The fire marshal issue was resolved, and 8,442 fans attended the game. Indiana would again reach 100 points as they defeated the Spartans 112 to 94. Dick had 23, Tom 21, Redenbaugh 20, and McGlocklin 18. Indiana would go to Northwestern and win by 10, as all starters were in double figures.

February 15 would bring one of those games that today's television play-by-play men call the game of the year. The Big Ten was loaded in 1965 with four of the top teams in the country: Michigan, Indiana, Illinois, and Minnesota were all very talented. In fact, Larry Cooper would say, "Years later, I would watch the NBA All-Star game and it looked like old home week. So many of the players were ones I played against in the Big Ten." It was number-1 Michigan against number-7 IU. To do this game and story justice, we will review some of the play-by-play.

Indiana would control the tip, but Michigan was the first to score.

Dick Van would hit a free throw. Remember that back then, if you were fouled and you weren't shooting, and it was before your team was in the bonus, you got one shot—really! McGlocklin's runner gave IU their first field goal, Cooper would hit a jumper, and Tom would bank one off the glass and IU was down 7 to 9. After a Michigan free throw, Cooper would gather in a rebound and dish it out to Tom, who would hit Dick underneath for 2 and it was 9 to 10, Michigan. Tom would hit a twisting layup to put IU ahead, 11 to 10, with 15 minutes to go in the first half. Cazzie Russell would hit for a 3-point, in those days a basket and a free throw. Tom would put back a Redenbaugh miss, and IU led, 19 to 18. A basket by Tom off a miss by Dick and a 12-foot hook shot by Cooper would put IU ahead, 23 to 20. With 9 minutes to go in the first half, Redenbaugh hit Tom for 2, and then Harden hit Tom for 2 and an IU lead of 29 to 26. Dick would be fouled by Russell and hit on one of two to tie the game at 30 points apiece. Harden would hit Dick for a 3-point play with 6 minutes to go, and IU led, 35 to 33. With a little over 2 minutes remaining in the first half, Dick hit 2 free throws to extend the IU lead to 42 to 38. Russell would counter with 2 free throws, and a Harden steal would lead to a Peyser basket which made it 48 to 42. Harden hit Tom underneath for 2, and IU led 50 to 44 at half.

Michigan, on a Russell free throw, would score first in the second half. IU countered with a McGlocklin jumper. Bill Buntin would tip in a missed shot and IU led, 55 to 53. Indiana would get another 3-point play from Dick as Tom would hit Dick with a pass underneath. Buntin would put back another miss, and Tom would take a rebound the length of the floor for a 22-foot jump shot, and IU led, 62 to 55. Another Buntin hook shot and with 10 minutes to go, it was IU ahead 64 to 61. A turn-around jump shot by Dick made it 70 to 65. Russell hit two free throws and it was 70 to 67. Tom would hit one of two free throws and IU led, 71 to 70. Redenbaugh would bank in a jumper to give the lead back to Indiana, 73 to 72.

This is where history gets blurred. Years later fans would say, knowing that IU led 81 to 74 with 1 minute 9 seconds to go in the game, that a Knight-coached team would not have lost. The myth is that Indiana under McCracken kept running and lost the lead, but as you will see, nothing could be further from the truth. Indiana, nursing a 2-point lead and having the ball, would call time. Branch would go with a 2-1-2 offense that blended to a 3-2 offense with McGlocklin at the top of the free-throw circle. Indiana would have the 2 men on the top go down and pick, and the players picked would rotate to the top. Indiana would pass the ball 21 times before Michigan, forgetting about McGlocklin, allowed him to catch pass 21 for a beautiful scooping layup and an IU lead of 76 to 72 with 3:40 to go. A Michigan miss and another 25 passes later, McGlocklin hit Tom for 2 underneath and an Indiana 78-to-72 lead with 2:28 left. Indiana would get the ball back, but as Al Harden was bringing the ball up, he was hit by three Michigan players and no foul was called, much to the displeasure of Hoosier fans as Cooper recalled, "Al got mugged by Cazzie."[6]

Michigan would score and draw closer to IU. Tom would hit Redenbaugh after 10 passes for a layup. Tom would go to the line with 1 minute to go and hit his first free throw to make it 81 to 74; however, he would miss his second. Buntin would then be fouled, hit his free throw, and miss his second. Michigan would rebound and score. Tom would gather in a rebound, be fouled, and miss the front end of a one and one. Michigan would hit a jumper, IU would travel, then a Buntin tip-in. Harden, bringing the ball up, would be trapped and fall to the ground. A jump ball was called and Michigan would control the tip. IU would foul Michigan, and Michigan would hit both free throws and a Harden shot at the buzzer was blocked. The game would end 81 to 81 in regulation and overtime would take place.

The first overtime tip would go to IU, and Tom would score a layup to make it 83 to 81. Michigan moments later would score off of a steal. Dick would foul out and McGlocklin would hit a jumper, and IU would go up, 85 to 83. Larry Cooper would hit one out of two free throws to push the lead to 3, 86 to 83. Redenbaugh would hit 2 free throws, and it was 88 to 84. Michigan would score and McGlocklin would counter with a basket and push the lead back up to 4. With 1 minute to go, Michigan would score, and then with just 36 seconds to go, Redenbaugh would hit

2 free throws. Indiana was now up 4 with 36 seconds to go. Michigan would be fouled and hit 2 free throws to trim IU's lead to 2. With 20 seconds to go in the game, Indiana would have the opportunity to put the game away with a breakaway layup. Peyser would be fouled and miss both free throws. Michigan would then miss a shot, but a Buntin tip-in at the buzzer would tie the score and send the game to double overtime.

In the second overtime, Michigan would score first at 3:29. Tom Van would drive and get fouled. Tom would hit one of two and the score would stand at 94 to 93. Tom would get fouled with 1:31 to go and miss the front end of a one and one, and the score would stand at 94 to 93. Tom would atone for the missed free throw by stealing the ball at half court and driving in for the go-ahead layup to give IU the lead, 95 to 94. Cazzie Russell would be fouled, hit both free throws, and put Michigan back on top, 96 to 95. Steve Redenbaugh would put up an 8-foot jump shot from the right side that would be blocked, and Michigan would hang on to win, 96 to 95. Indiana had dropped a game they should have won, and a team that would shoot 77% from the free throw line would miss 15 free throws in the game. Dave McCracken would say years later, "Jon McGlocklin would tell me that he thought that if Indiana would have made the NCAA Tournament, he was not sure how far they would have gone. Because they had fought so hard and given so much, he wasn't sure how much they had left."[7] In the Michigan game most of the missed free throws were off the front of the rim, which would indicate tired legs.

McCracken was visibly upset after the game. Branch would chew out the team after the game in the locker room. "My God, boys, you sure let one get away tonight," McCracken roared in front of a locker room full of reporters. Visibly shaken, Branch railed against a litany of Hoosier errors. He complained about his team's free throw shooting, their sloppy passing, and their untimely shooting. "We had them. We had them cold, and we let them get away," he whispered, shaking his head. Then perked up a bit and added, "But keep your chins up, hold your heads high, you're a good ball club. Forget about practice tomorrow, and think this one over in your own minds."[8]

Indiana would rebound and, scoring 100 points for the sixth time on the year, defeat Wisconsin, 100 to 87, with great scoring balance led by Dick's 26, Tom's 23, Redenbaugh's 4, Cooper's 13, and McGlocklin's 12. Indiana would lose the next two on the road to Purdue and Minnesota. Indiana would have three games left. IU next hosted Ohio State and for the seventh and last time of the year scored 100 or more points in defeating the Buckeyes, 110 to 90.

*Ticket from last game Branch coached (Murphy Collection).*

The day was March 6. News had leaked that Branch had announced earlier in the week that this season, his twenty-fourth at Indiana, would be his last. Fittingly, his last home game would be against Purdue—the team that his son, Dave, would say that if Dad could win only one game a year, it would be against Purdue. Branch, however, suffering from poor health, would be confined to a hospital bed. The doctor would tell Mary Jo and Dave, "We have to let him coach this game. He's rolling over and walking around the room. If we don't let him coach, he's going to die right here and now."⁹ So Branch would coach.

McCracken was set to coach his last home game and, as it turned out, his last game. He was too ill to travel to Wisconsin for Indiana's last game of the 1965 Season. Indiana was 17 and 5 at this point and 7 and 5 in the Big Ten. Saturday night, March 6, at 7:30 p.m., fans would settle into their four-dollar seats to witness the seven seniors' last home game and Branch McCracken's last game at IU.

Indiana would start Tom and Dick Van Arsdale, Jon McGlocklin, Larry Cooper, and Steve Redenbaugh against Purdue. The game would start off perfectly as Cooper tipped the ball to Redenbaugh, who returned the ball back to Cooper underneath for two and IU led 2 to nothing. A jump ball would follow and Cooper would win the tip-over to Dick, who would hit a jumper, and IU would lead, 4 to 0. Purdue's star, Dave Schellhase, would hit a couple of baskets to tie the game. Tom Van would hit a jumper off the glass and IU led, 7 to 5. Redenbaugh would cut across the lane and bank in a jumper at 16:33, and the Hoosiers led, 9 to 6. Tom Van would hit a long-range jumper at the 16-minute mark, and Indiana led, 11 to 6. Cooper would hit a jumper and it was 13 to 8 with 15:33 to go. Dick Van would put back his own missed shot and with 14 minutes to go, IU led, 15 to 9. With 13 minutes left in the first half, McGlocklin would hit a jumper to put Indiana up, 19 to 11. Dick would hit 2 free throws and after a few Schellhase points, Indiana led, 23 to 21, with 8:50 left in the first half. Purdue would take the lead, 33 to 31, with another Schellhase jumper with 3:38 to go in the half. Peyser would hit a free throw, then a Redenbaugh steal would lead to a Harden layup, and IU was back on top, 34 to 33. Harden would then steal the inbound pass and score another lay-up. Both teams would trade baskets and the score would stand at 40 to 38. Tom Van would score on a 3-point play and Indiana led, 43 to 38. Purdue would come back and, with 30 seconds to go in the half, Tom hit a baseline jumper on a pass from Johnson and Indiana led, 45 to 44.

It had finally come—the last half of basketball Branch would ever coach. Indiana would win the tip and, after misses by both teams, Redenbaugh would score and IU was up by 3. With 17 minutes left, Cooper would score and the Hoosiers led, 51 to 44. Dick would pass to Tom for a 3-point play, and Cooper would hit a shot with 15 minutes to go, and the Hoosiers led, 58 to 49. Dick Van would have two steals that would result in baskets by Redenbaugh and Dick himself. Purdue would score and with 10 minutes left, IU led, 69 to 62. Indiana would lead, 76 to 69, with 5:37 remaining. Indiana would score on a half hook by Jon McGlocklin and with 4:47 left in the game, the Hoosiers would lead, 78 to 71. Purdue would come back to close the gap to 3, 78 to 75. Dick would hit a left-handed layup to push the score to 80 to 75. Cooper would hit and it was now 82 to 75. Schellhase would score and a Tom Van Arsdale tip-in off a Hoosier miss gave Indiana an 84-to-77 lead with 2:10 left in the game. The game was coming to an end, and Indiana was controlling the ball when Dick saw Al Harden on the other side of the court cut toward the basket for a wide-open layup. Dick Van Arsdale would hit two free throws at the end to put a cap on the game, and the season, 90 to 79. McCracken's career had come to an end in a wonderfully victorious fashion.

*Branch's last game was a home victory over Purdue, 90–79.*
*Here, Jon McGlocklin scores 2 points in the second*
*half as Steve Redenbaugh looks on.*

McCracken was walking off the court when he was beckoned back. With his arm around Al Harden, Branch would listen at center court as a plaque to him was read to all in attendance. McCracken was flanked by players Redenbaugh, Harden, McGlocklin, the Vans, Cooper, and Peyser. He adjusted his glasses as the emotion of the moment showed through, and he walked off the court a living legend of Indiana basketball. The Hoosiers would be led on the evening by Tom Van Arsdale's 19, followed by McGlocklin's 16, Dick Van Arsdale and Larry Cooper's 14 each, Redenbaugh's 13, Harden's 9, Peyser's 3, and Johnson's 2 in front of 9,023 grateful fans.

McCracken's last team would have a record of 19 wins and 5 losses. It would be the third-highest victory total on a season in his career, and Branch would leave the home court in Bloomington in 1965 the same way he had left his very first game back in 1938 at home: a winner.

*Branch with his seven seniors from his last team 1964 – 65*
*(L – R, Front Row: Larry Cooper, Steve Redenbaugh,*
*Branch McCracken, Al Harden, Jon McGlocklin,*
*Second Row: Ron Peyser, Tom Van Arsdale,*
*Dick Van Arsdale (Courtesy Larry Cooper)*

# Chapter 20

## BRANCH AFTER INDIANA BASKETBALL

B RANCH HAD COACHED HIS LAST GAME AT IU: A 90-TO-79 WIN OVER Purdue. The win over the Boilermakers would be McCracken's twenty-eighth against only fifteen losses. Dave McCracken would say, "If you told Dad he could win only one game all year, the game he would want to win would be against Purdue, no question about it."[1]

Indiana as a team would have one more game remaining against Wisconsin at Madison, but Branch was too ill to travel and see his team finish the season on a positive note with a 92-to-73 win.

Branch would submit a brief but moving letter of resignation saying, "My association with Indiana University as a student, player, and coach has been a long and rewarding one. I am sincerely grateful to those alumni, friends, faculty, administrators, coaches, and especially to the fine young men who have played for me, giving me the opportunity to serve Indiana University as head coach to the best of my ability. However, I feel that I must now submit my resignation and request I be relieved of my duties in accordance with the terms of my contract."[2]

An editorial appeared in *The Herald-Telephone* after Branch's resignation that was a fitting tribute to Branch McCracken: "We know there will be other bright spots for the Hurryin' Hoosiers because our state knows no peer in the development of superior hoopsters. Like Stan Musial, Red Grange, or Jack Dempsey, however, it will take super effort on the parts of future IU coaches to match the record of the 'Big Bear,' 'The Sheriff,' 'The pride of Monrovia.'"[3]

Branch in the summer of 1963 had started a basketball camp in Angola, Indiana. This camp would become an outlet for him upon his retirement from Indiana basketball, keeping him involved in the game he loved. His son Dave would say, however, that "Dad was truly never happy being away from basketball, especially at Indiana."[4]

McCracken would stay involved at Indiana with his office in the physical education department, with the job of supervising student teachers around the state. This job would afford Branch the opportunity to travel the state where he had a vest network of people. Former players who were now coaches themselves, students of Indiana, friends, and fans would make up this web of McCracken connections. Players like Tom Bolyard and Jade Butcher of IU Rose Bowl fame would stop by McCracken's office for coffee, cokes, donuts, and conversation

Tom Bolyard would say that four or five times a year, he and Branch would go golfing. Bolyard would say, "Branch was a terrible golfer, just awful. We would be playing, and he would hit a bad shot. He would just shake his head and say as we were walking 'this game ruins a perfectly good walk.'"[5] Jade Butcher would say, "He was a great man and a great coach. I would love to have played for that man."[6]

McCracken would win his last battle off the court as he secured the Indiana head basketball job for his former assistant head coach, captain, and former player, Lou Watson.

Branch would live just five short years after retiring from coaching at Indiana. He would die in an Indianapolis hospital on June 4, 1970, of a heart ailment just five days short of his sixty-second birthday.

Good friend Wilson Thrasher would say, "We were really friends. I talked to him on the telephone when he was in the hospital in Indianapolis two days before he died. He was strong to the end—he knew it was coming. He knew the outcome. No fumbling/stumbling about it, he was a man. Outstanding—I wish everyone was like him. I would like to be respected like he was."[7]

Indiana would move into Assembly Hall in 1971 from the New Fieldhouse that had been the Hoosiers' home for the last 11 years and the venue of Branch's last coaching efforts.

Saturday afternoon at 2:00, December 18, 1971, Indiana would host Notre Dame and hold a dedication ceremony of Assembly Hall and the naming of Branch McCracken Memorial Basketball Floor.

Chancellor Herman Wells presented a painting and made remarks about his old classmate and friend Branch. President Ryan then presented a tribute and bestowed the name of the court. Mary Jo and Dave McCracken unveiled the plaque honoring Branch, and Mary Jo said a few words to the more than 17,00 fans there not only to see the game, but to honor the legend who was Branch McCracken.

A fitting tribute would be placed in the program that day, entitled, "Big Mac A Winner and A Legend." The tribute was written by a person who would remain nameless, calling themselves just an old friend. The words that follow are but an excerpt of that tribute:

Branch McCracken was many things to many people. He was one of those rare individuals who loom larger than life size—whose achievements, color, and personality bid to lend him a legendary hue within his own time. Branch would snort at the term, but it was probably what politicians now refer to as charisma.

To many, the McCracken memory is of a coach, and a fabulously successful one. The record permits no equivocation on that point. To others, it was McCracken the showman, although it all came naturally and was part of the business of winning—which was Mac's business. Home games in the Old Fieldhouse were a replay of the good guys versus the bad guys. What fans of that era can never forget, is the handsome 6 foot 4 strapping figure, white hair gleaming, as he reared to his feet, face livid, and pointing with an imperious finger in righteous wrath at some impossible call by an errant official.

McCracken was a genuine, fierce competitor and his rages set a mood, an atmosphere that created battling teams with a killer instinct. McCracken himself would say, "How can I build a team that fights for me if I don't fight for them?

In return, those who played for Branch carried a blazing personal loyalty that knew no bounds. It was and is a mark of pride for all to say, 'I played for Branch McCracken at Indiana.' For most, it was an extension of the father-son relationship. Branch felt a personal responsibility to both the athlete and his parents.

McCracken would say, "When parents entrust me with their son for four years, I owe it to them, and to him, to give them back a better man."

Branch was a master recruiter. Big, handsome, and colorful, he had the common touch. He was just plain folks, thoroughly Hoosier in the classic pattern, and his reputation, sincerity, and dedication to the old-fashioned virtues of effort and sacrifice, coupled with his drawl and bent for homespun philosophy, made him as much a favorite in the family living room as on the far-ranging banquet circuit.

To a lot of people, Mac was the big fellow at the speaker's platform who could make them laugh and cry sometimes in the same sentence. He was a star there also, although he characterized himself as a triple-threat speaker: "Stumble, fumble, and sit down."

To others, he was an apostle of basketball, whose doctrine of the fast-break dominated an era through example, coaching clinics over three continents, and a best-seller book, "Indiana Basketball."

To everyone, he was an example of the self-made man, a farm boy of a big, poor but proud family, which never took time to consider itself underprivileged. A high school star from such humble beginnings that his first taste of the game was with an inflated pig bladder tossed at a hoop nailed to a barn, an All-American at Indiana, where he discovered football in three years as a standout end. He never lost sight of where he started, the people from which he sprung, and the principles implanted in him.

He was a bear of a man with courage to match. When that big heart, strained, no doubt, by the tensions and pressures of his demanding craft, first began to falter, the wise course would have been to retire. Instead, he stuck to it. It probably cost him his life at much too early an age. So, he passed on into legend, famed, honored, and respected. Of all the accolades, Branch McCracken of Indiana, would be enough and probably would have pleased him most.[8]

These words were a perfect tribute to the man, and it is most fitting that the author named him- or herself as "just an old friend"—almost as if the words were written by Indiana University herself.

*Branch always coaching*

# Chapter 21

## Stories About the Sheriff

*I have had the opportunity to speak with many individuals who remember McCracken well. The last chapter in this book is a collection of those stories gathered from 1989 to 2013 about Branch from the people who knew him best.*

My favorite story about Branch came from his son, Dave. "Dad was in the hospital and the doctor had told him he would have to quit coaching or he would die. The doctor came out and told Mom and I what he had told Dad. We both were afraid to go into his room, but we went in anyway. To our surprise, Dad was in a great mood. We asked him if he understood what the doctor had said, and he said with a smile, 'Yes, how many people know how they are going to die.'" Indiana basketball ran deep in Branch's blood.

Dave would also recall the time when Branch charged onto the court to dispute a call. The official looked at Branch and told him it would cost him a technical foul for every step it took him to get back to Indiana's bench. Branch looked to the bench and summoned two players to come out and carry him back to the bench. No technical was assessed.

*Dick Sparks of Bloomington would be McCracken's only
recruit the year after Indiana was hit with sanctions.*

Dick Sparks would say that "Branch's deep-throated voice was a huge asset to him. When giving the referees a piece of his mind, he could belt out his complaint while not looking at the referee, thus avoiding a technical foul."

Larry Cooper would add, "We played in the Fieldhouse, and the floor was set up knee-level. Coach had a towel and he wrapped the end of that thing with tape. He would slap that towel on the court and it didn't matter what kind of noise was in the Fieldhouse, he would slap that towel down and look at you and tell you what he wanted right now." Cooper would also talk about the famous seatbelt that McCracken appeared with in a newspaper picture entitled "Hoosier Point Saver": "There was a time that they had just passed a regulation about coaches jumping up and yelling at the referees. Somebody installed a seatbelt on the bench for Branch. Branch didn't think it was as funny as the rest of them. Even though pictures were taken with Branch wearing it and smiling, that seatbelt was gone the next day."

One referee found a unique way of controlling Branch's rants. When asked how he got Branch, who was vehemently objecting to a call, to sit down quickly, Official Jim Enright said, "Nothing to it. I just said, 'Now Branch, you've made your point and you'd better sit down. You know, this game's on television and your fly is open.'"

Jim Schooley would tell how "when Mac got a little too excited about a call, Ernie Andress would grab his belt to keep him from wandering too far out on the court and getting a technical foul." Schooley also talked about the McCracken practices. "We spent a lot of work on the backboards, the big guys did. The idea was we would have one big guy on one side and one big guy on the other side of the bucket, and instead of trying to put the ball in the basket, you just put the ball over the rim to the other guy. We ran and ran in practice. Mac would say, 'My game is a speed game, and we may not take as high a percentage shot as the other team, but we are going to get a lot more shots than they do.'"

Dick Sparks would talk about Branch's intensity: "Branch and Lou made you work hard in practice. If you were slacking, be ready for the wrath of God."

Ray Pavy said, "Branch had such a presence. One time years after I had played, I was sitting with Herman Wells at a basketball game. We were at Assembly Hall watching Knight's team. Knight was going crazy on a call. President Wells said to me, 'There's not much difference between Knight and the Bear—Knight has nothing on Branch.'"

Pavy would add, "Branch's greatest talent was making you believe you were the best shooter in the world."

He also summed up how many players felt about Branch: "Branch loved all his boys. He was a big bear, but he was mellow inside. After I was hurt, Branch, with Herman Wells, made sure I could continue to go to IU and graduate. President Wells would make sure every one of my classes were on the first floor (except Science because of the labs), so I could get to class. I was the special-needs student at IU at the time."

One of Branch's nicknames—"Doc"—came from his youth and his desire to become a veterinarian; however, it seemed to apply to McCracken's care for his players as well. Tom Van Arsdale would recall, "When Dick and I were in our junior year, we both got sick with the flu. We were living in the SAE Fraternity house, and Branch came over to the house unannounced and walked up the flight of stairs to our room carrying a bag of groceries. Inside were all sorts of things that one would likely take to fight off the flu—it was filled with juices, et cetera."

Jim Schooley told of a time when, as a sophomore, he was eating with the team. "We had filet mignon and toast. The waiter asked if there was anything he could get for me, and I said I would like a glass of milk. Mac saw that and said, 'Don't you be doing that, it's very hard to digest. Don't you be drinking milk.' I thought that was funny because I had lived on milk since I was a kid."

*Max Walker was McCracken's last recruit out of*
*Wisconsin and Indiana's MVP in 1966.*

Max Walker would tell of Branch and Mary Jo's support upon the crib death of his son. "Branch and Mary Jo came up and said to me that they wanted to help me. They knew it was a very hard time, and as a student I had no money to get my son back to Milwaukee—that they would take care of all funeral expenses. That meant so much to me."

Walker also remembered eating with Branch and the experiences that would bring. "I had never heard of persimmon pudding, so Branch gave me some and said not to take too much because it was so sweet. Well, I took too much, a really big piece, and it was so sweet." Laughing, Walker recalled Branch looking at him and saying, "That's why I am the coach and you're the player." Walker would go on to say, "We would go to Branch's house for a cookout, and I never saw a streak come off the grill so fast. You could have put a fork in it and it would have mooed. I liked my steak well done and now, to this day, I like my steak rare."

Former player Pete Obremskey recalled Branch's benevolence. "Branch was responsible for paying seven years of my education, so to me, he walked on water. Of course, when I was playing for him, I didn't feel that way."[1]

Indiana great, Walt Bellamy, valued the relationship he had with Coach McCracken. "Coach McCracken touched all student athletes. I felt prepared. Did he holler and throw chairs? No, but he certainly was effective in preparing men to play basketball and to be successful in life."[2]

The *Indiana Daily Student* talked about McCracken as a player: "Height, ranginess and cleverness, the three attributes of a good center, are so manifest in Branch McCracken, that he already is one of the leading members of the squad. He has all the natural attributes of a good netman, coach Dean believes, and is expected to bear watching in spite of his experience." "McCracken's drive, long frame and keen eye for the loop caused him to be feared by all opposing pivot men. His strong suit is his ability to get the tip-off and to get through the guards for many follow-up shots."[3]

The senior manager preseason report on McCracken in 1930 would state of Branch, "Branch McCracken, husky offensive threat, is expected to handle the center position with ease this year. Although slightly larger than the average hardwood player, McCracken finds little difficulty in puzzling the defensive tactics of the offense and has shown considerable ability at scoring points on follow-up shots."[4]

Former player Lou Watson commented, "As a player, Branch kept the weight off you. He'd run you to death."

McCracken would tell the following story about himself. After a game, a fan asked McCracken, "Why did they call a technical foul on Indiana, coach?" McCracken would reply, "Indiana had too many men on the floor." The fan asked McCracken, "Who was the sixth man?" McCracken would respond, "Me."

*All-American Bill Garrett*

Speaking about recruiting Bill Garrett, McCracken would tell the *Indianapolis News*, "There's no rule against colored athletes, but somebody has to be the first to use them. It's going to be me." McCracken would tell the *LaFayette Journal and Courier*, "It wasn't as hard a thing for me as it was for Bill. All the pressure was on him, but he was an exceptional guy. He handled discrimination on and off the floor without changing expression."[5]

Bill Garrett would say of Branch, "He made you grow up real fast just by the way he handled the players. He had something about him that made it very easy on all the players as far as getting themselves ready. I think it was one of the greatest attributes he had as a coach."[6]

Archie Dees talked about McCracken's leadership, saying, "Mac was definitely a leader. He led every player, every person, that came in contact with him to greater heights than they could ever hope to achieve. He was a born leader."[7]

*Branch and Ernie Andres watch Indiana win its second championship, March 17, 1953.*

Ernie Andres remembered Branch's impact on the team from his very first year as a coach. "I was Mac's first captain. It was obvious he intended to win at Indiana. He had a winning attitude about him. He didn't believe in doing anything halfway. Everybody that played for Branch respected him. He would work you as hard as anybody yet at the same time he would do anything for you to try to help you, and it didn't just mean on the basketball court, but in school or in life in general."[8]

Bobby Leonard of the '53 championship team recalled, "Branch had a way about him. Branch was a winner and he instilled winning into the ball players, there's no doubt about it. There wasn't a night that you went on the floor that you weren't ready to tear someone apart. You went out there to win a ballgame—that was Branch. With Branch, you had such great admiration for him, and we were so close to him that you didn't want to feel in your own mind that you had let him down."[9]

Bill Garrett would add, "He had a solid way about him. His mannerism demanded respect. The overall respect he had from his players was amazing."[10]

Former teammate and longtime friend Jim Strickland knew a very aggressive Branch. "He was the most aggressive man I ever met in my life. He liked to go at it and go at it fast."[11]

McCracken's coach and Indiana Hall of Famer Everett Dean said of Branch, "Mac loved the game and he lived it. He had quite a spirit. He was an easy man to coach because of his attitude."[12]

Jim Strickland recalled, "His biggest concern was his boys. He worried more about his kids on his team—more than any coach I have ever known. He would follow them after they got out of school, and he was a huge help to them."[13]

All-American center Don Schlundt would say of Branch, "Without Branch, I would not be who I am today. He made me a better person. It was just the way you respected the man."[14]

Dees remembered Branch's use of psychology about whomever he would play against next. "He would walk up to me and say, 'This guy is tough. He's strong.' He used this on me, telling me he didn't want me to get hurt. He would start this on Wednesday and by Saturday, I couldn't wait to get out there and get a look at this guy. I really wanted to get at him. I was really ready to play. The crazy thing was that he did this so well that it not only worked my sophomore and junior years, but I would listen even as a senior. I would always listen to him."[15]

Long-time friend Bill Unsworth told of Branch's deep competitive nature with a story of how hard he would take a loss. "He had been beaten by Minnesota at Minnesota by one point. On the plane coming back from Minnesota, he would say, 'My goodness, if you could just get beat by 30 or 32 points, you could go to sleep at night with no stress, realizing that you had a club that wasn't going anywhere. It would make all the difference in the world sleeping or not sleeping.' The following year, Indiana was invited to the University of Cincinnati to dedicate their new Fieldhouse. Well, the day of the game at noon, there was a lunch given by the University of Cincinnati in honor of Branch for playing on that Monrovia team that won back-to-back championships in the High School Tri-State Tourney that was held in Cincinnati each year. As fate would have it, Cincinnati would beat IU that day by 32 points. Mac got on the team bus and said, 'My, my, if you could just get beat by one point, you would know you had something. You would hate the one-point loss, but you could be full of pride and you would know you had something. How can anyone sleep if you get beat by 32?'" Unsworth would go on to say that "everyone who knew Mac felt like they knew him well, that they were his best friend."[16]

Jim Strickland recalled how Branch inspired everyone. "We were at Illinois and a group of us had gone down to the locker room before the game. We would leave when the boys came in to get dressed. We didn't notice that one of our party had fallen asleep in the corner of the locker room behind the lockers. We were standing outside, and we heard Branch pounding on the table and firing the boys up. The next thing you know, the team burst through the doors and following them was our friend, as ready as the boys. If Mac had given him a suit, he would have played." Strickland continued, "I never knew Mac to do anything he didn't think was in the best interest of IU and his boys. He was so completely dedicated to Indiana University."[17]

McCracken was asked about raising the height of the basket, to which he responded, "Don't raise the basket, that makes it tough on the little six-foot-three fellow. Instead, make the hoop smaller."[18]

During the 1949–50 season, Indiana would begin the season with ten straight wins. Dr. Marvin Christie would recall the game that broke the streak and McCracken's reaction. "The game was tied at 67, and Michigan had the ball underneath their basket with six seconds left. Michigan would inbound the ball, and after a couple of seconds, shoot and miss. The ball bounced out deep into the backcourt. When Michigan recovered the rebound, I looked up and there were still six seconds left on the clock. Michigan shot again and finally scored as the buzzer went off. A good fifteen seconds must have transpired. Branch leaped up from the bench to rush to the scorer's table. The official scorer jumped up and ran across the court as Branch approached, yelling that Indiana had been robbed. The Michigan coaches approached Branch. By that time, Branch had taken us off the court and we were headed to the locker room. The Michigan coaches couldn't have been nicer. They told Branch we will play an over-time, but Branch would hear none of it. Then they said they wouldn't count the game and we would play again at a neutral site, but again, Branch said no. When Branch got upset, you couldn't control him. He just wasn't going to play them again, he was so mad. I think he thought the loss might motivate us even more the rest of the season. We ended up third in the Big Ten that year."

On December 29 and 30 in 1949, Indiana traveled to Indianapolis to play in the Hoosier Classic. Before the game, Sam Miranda asked Marvin Christie a question about a class he was taking in which Dr. Christie excelled. Dr. Christie recalled, "We were in the locker room and all of a sudden these big six-foot lockers in the center began crashing down in our direction. It took a few of us players to keep them from falling down. Then we hear Branch from the other side of the lockers bellow out, 'We don't talk academics right before a game.'"

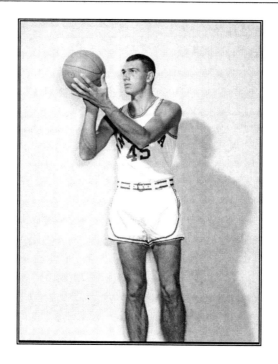

*Tom Bolyard*

Tom Bolyard would recall that Branch had social media before twitter. "There were five or six coffee shops on the square in downtown Bloomington, and Branch would go to each one, sit down, and have coffee with everyone. He built up quite a network. As a player, you could not go anywhere or do anything in the community without Branch knowing about it. People would call Branch up and say, 'Hey, so-and-so are here—should they be?' and if we weren't supposed to be there, Branch would be there shortly after. He just knew everything. We as players knew you couldn't get away with anything." Although Branch didn't want the players talking academics before the games, he wanted his players to do well in the classroom. Bolyard said that Branch would give the professors of his players three-by-five cards, and they were to write down if a player missed class or if any of them were having any kind of problem in class.

All of the players would remember with fondness how much Branch cared about them and how hard he would fight for them. Dr. Christie remembered a time in February of 1950 when Indiana traveled to

Chicago to take on Northwestern. "This was during the time when Jackie Robinson was breaking the color line in baseball, as Bill Garrett was doing the same thing for Big Ten basketball. Everyone was on edge, so we tried to stay in the student unions as much as possible. However, on this trip we were staying in Chicago at the Morrison Hotel. When we walked into the lobby, the manager of the hotel came out from behind the front desk into the lobby area and stopped us as we entered. He put his finger onto Bill Garrett's chest and told Branch that 'You're not staying here with *him*.' Branch got so mad we had to try to hold him back as Branch launched at the manager. The manager got scared and jumped behind the front desk. Well, Branch went over the desk after him. We were trying to hold Branch back—we didn't want him to get into trouble and us be without a coach. Ernie Andres called another hotel, and we would walk three blocks to the Blackstone and stay there. Branch was bound and determined that Bill Garrett would be treated fairly."

*Vern Payne was one of Branch's last recruits.*

Vern Payne talked about coming from humble beginnings and how kind and wonderful Dr. Robert Milisen and the coaches were to both his mother and himself when they went out to dinner on his recruiting trip. "Coach McCracken came into the Michigan City locker room, where I remembered this huge, iconic man with white hair who was very kind and gracious telling me [in what Vern said turned the tables in IU's favor] that he was going to keep the hurryin' in the Hoosiers. They were going to run, run, run and use their 2-2-1 press. I knew it would be to my advantage to play at IU with this up-tempo game that I loved."

Payne told a story that he felt best typified who McCracken and Watson were as people. This happened while Watson was coaching IU, but Payne would say that Watson had learned this philosophy from Branch. "Coach McCracken was an icon, just a fine man, and he had instilled in Coach Watson these values. I was a sophomore starting in a game when we, IU, got a steal. I was way out in front on a fast break when my teammate [Payne was way too much the gentleman to name names], took the ball and instead of passing, drove all the way down for a layup. Nothing was said during the game, but the next day in practice, instead of going to the court, Coach Watson had us go to the film room. There he had the projector right at the spot of the steal. He would show the play over and over again with myself out front and no lead pass. As Coach Watson showed the film, he became very emotional. He would stop the film and say, 'As long as I'm the basketball coach here at Indiana, this will never happen again. I don't care who it is, whether you're black or white, you are teammates playing for the Red and White of Indiana. Whoever is out front gets the ball.' Coach Watson would then send us all home." Amused, Payne would recall that after that day, "I almost had to have my head in a swivel, so many passes were coming my way. That's one thing Coach Watson learned from Coach McCracken. Coach McCracken was a wonderful man."

Branch would begin every preseason with a cross-country run for his basketball players. Branch loved this run much more than his players did, and sometimes Branch would really get into it. Dr. Christie told of a time when Branch drove his car behind the runners. "'Mule Train' was a big song back then, and Branch would drive behind us with the window to his car down singing—almost shouting—the song 'Mule Train,' singing, 'Crack that whip!' He would ease his car up to the last runner and, with his bumper, bump into the runners' calves—all in fun and not to hurt anyone, but we would all look over our shoulders to make sure we weren't last."

Dave McCracken recalled that his parents had met through one of Branch's teammates who was coaching football at Muncie High School at the time. "Dad needed a ride home and Mom was asked if she would mind giving Dad a ride home. Dad would then ask Mom if she wanted to go with him to Selma, Indiana, where Mom was from. He was going up there to referee a game. From there, their romance was on. For Christmas that year, Dad gave Mom a Spaulding basketball rule book, and his picture was in many of the pages. Mom was impressed and I think from that point on, Dad was in with Mom."

*Branch with Dick and Tom Van Arsdale and their parents,*
*Raymond and Hilda Van Arsdale (Bob Gomel, Courtesy of Life Magazine)*

When asked what Branch stood for, Tom Van Arsdale replied, "Just from the standpoint of what he stood for—the tradition that he had developed over the years at Indiana. The way he treated me was an influence on me, and I think it taught me that it is important to treat your fellow man with respect and kindness, and you can still be effective doing that."[19]

Tom Bolyard would add, "He was like a father. Between classes, if I had a break, I went to his office, have a coke, and talk, not only about basketball, but schoolwork, life, what I was going to do when I got out of school. I tell you, he was just like a father to me. I probably couldn't have made it without him."

Bobby "Slick" Leonard would say of McCracken, "He took me as a wild kid off the streets of Terre Haute and taught me a lot of values. I had never been baptized—Branch took me to a church and had me baptized when I was 19 years old. You don't get any greater feeling for a man than I have for Branch McCracken. There is no greater feeling."[20]

Rayl recalled getting married in 1966 and sending Branch and Mary Jo an invitation. "I didn't really know if he would be able to come or not, but that day, there he was with Mary Jo, sitting right up front with a huge smile on his face. It meant a lot."

Many of the players would remember that every year before the first game, Branch would take them to the Crane Navy Depot and they would have a big dinner in the Officers' Club. Branch had been a navy officer, so he would get them into the club. According to all, he was dashing in his uniform.

Larry Cooper remembered how Branch helped him through a rough time in 1965. "At the start of my senior year, a good friend who I played with for two years at Hutchinson Junior College at Kansas was killed in a car crash. Coach released me from the final drill before the start of fall practice and allowed me to return to Kansas City for my friend's funeral. This may sound like a minor thing, but it meant a lot to me at the time."

*Jimmy Rayl.*

"To this day, I'm one of the most prompt guys because of Branch," Rayl would say. "Branch had 'Lombardi Time' before Lombardi. If you weren't fifteen minutes early, you were late. I remember one time Walt Ballamy wasn't there on Branch's time, and we left on our way to the airport without Walt. Walt would pass our bus and big Walter would be waving as they passed. He had gotten a ride with a friend, but if you were late, didn't matter who you were—we left."

Several players recalled Branch wearing his gray T-shirt and gray pants (the forerunner to sweatpants), standing on the court greeting each player before practice, saying hi to each, and giving just a personal comment to let you know you were important to him as a person. "We were his kids."

The Big Bear, Branch, was famous for yelling at a player, "Get up— you're not hurt!" Rayl said, "One day at practice, Dave Porter fouled me on a fast break and sent me flying into those goose-neck goal posts we had. I went sliding down it. Branch rushed over to see if I was alright. He didn't say 'Get up!' that day."

Tom Van Arsdale would also comment on Branch's famous saying of "Get up—you're not hurt!": "Branch was a rough-and-tumble man. … One day in practice, the team was running fast-break drills and he got run over by one of us, I don't remember who it was. As Branch was flat on his back, the entire team circled him and yelled, 'Get up—you are not hurt!' As it turned out, he was injured and we all felt terrible. Branch was sure a great man, and we all loved him."

Ray Pavy talked about Branch's coaching genius. "It was a remarkable thing that two coaching greats, McCracken and Wooden, came from the same area. They both understood the game so well, and both used a press on defense to speed up the game—McCracken a man-to-man press and Wooden a zone press—but their idea of speeding up the game was due to their feeling that 'our talent will beat your talent.'"

McCracken himself would say in a 1956 interview, "We've won a lot of basketball games in the past 18 years, and what I tell my boys is when you put that Indiana uniform on, it's just like waving a red flag. The other coach doesn't have to give his team much of a pep talk. He just has to say, 'We're playing Indiana tonight, and those boys come up for it.'"[21]

Bolyard remembered a McCracken strategy for games. "He would come in and say, 'Jim, I need twenty shots out of you and, Bolyard, twenty shots out of you.' Then he would turn to Dick and Tom Van Arsdale, 'I need twelve shots out of both of you,' and so on. That was part of his game-day strategy."

Archie Dees, the first two-time Big Ten MVP, would say of McCracken, "He was just a born leader. It was an honor to play for him. It was the type of situation that you never had to question, 'was he telling you the right thing?' Whatever I was told, I would do without any reservation, and I think that is one of the most important things in being a coach."

Branch was not only a coach, but in those days, he was also a schedule maker. Marvin Christie remembered, "Branch was helpful in getting classes arranged. We had to be done by two, so Branch would make sure we got the early classes that would start at 7:30 to be sure we were there for practice."

In the forties through the sixties, Branch was larger than life in Indiana. Former teammate and lifelong friend Jim Strickland talked about a recruiting trip Branch had planned for the two of them. "Mac said, 'We are going to sneak over to the Elks Club and get a bite to eat, then go over to the gym and sneak a look at this kid, and then sneak back over to Owensville and spend the night.' I said, 'Great, they're looking for us.' So we sneak into the Elks Club, and the whole dining room stood up and they played the IU fight song. Very sneaky."[22]

Tom Van Arsdale said of McCracken, "Branch was a 'run, run, run' type of coach. Get the ball up the floor as fast as you could. Branch's number one criteria was, you put out the whole game. To play for Branch—for this system that you had watched on television for years and years—it was one of those things you think you are going to win just because Indiana has always won, and Branch instilled that in people."[23]

Jim Schooley remembered being recruited by Branch. "I remember we were in the living room. We lived in an old house there in Auburn, Indiana. Mac really impressed my mother. My dad had died a couple of years earlier. My mom had very little income, and Mac was very much the gentleman. He said Indiana had an excellent chemistry department, and he would make sure that I would go to school when I came down, which he did. My mother said, 'Isn't he a fine-looking man?'"

When playing for a demanding coach like McCracken, things were not always that smooth. Once, Bobby Leonard was called into McCracken's office for one of the famous McCracken talks to straighten a player out. "He called me in his office. He told me, 'When we get through, if I ever have to call you in again, I'll lock the door, and only one of us will come out.'" Leonard promised he would change, but before he left, Leonard said he "stopped at the door and said, 'I guess I know which one of us will come out,' and then I ran down the hall." Leonard would add, however, "He was a great guy and a great man."[24]

Rayl and Tom Van Arsdale both remembered that Branch's health problems would surface during their years at IU and he hid it the best he could from the players.

Marvin Christie said that Branch was 100% dedicated to IU. He remembered Branch saying, "I can win a national championship with players from Indiana."

Dick Enberg would say of Branch, "To the core, there was no doubt that Branch was an Indiana man."[25]

The 1966 Indiana basketball guide would pay a lasting tribute to Coach McCracken entitled "Thanks, Mac." It began:

> The start of a new era in Indiana basketball prompts a look back at the McCracken Era of IU. A peek at those golden years at Indiana and the record achieved by those exciting Hoosier teams emphasizes the debt of gratitude basketball fans of the state and nation owe to the Sheriff.
>
> For example: Two National Collegiate Championships; three Big Ten titles and a share of a fourth; teams which placed either first or second in the Big Ten 12 of his 24 seasons; teams which placed out of the top five in the Conference only four times in 24 years; a 354–174 winning performance and a 210–116 mark in Big Ten play; a career

coaching record at both Indiana and Ball State of 457–215;
a winning margin over every other Big Ten team (Chicago,
6–0; Michigan, 24–9; Michigan State, 20–7; Wisconsin,
25–10; Purdue, 28–15; Northwestern, 21–10; Iowa, 24–16;
Ohio State, 27–17; Minnesota, 19–16; Illinois, 19–17).

It was a time of great excitement, of great play, and
not least great coaching. All eras must come to an end and
there will be other great days ahead. But none will forget
the great contributions of Branch McCracken to Indiana
University, its basketball program and basketball fans
everywhere; from them, "Thanks, Mac. Well done."[26]

His son Dave would say of his dad, "He was a man, and all that
means. He was strong. His word meant something. He was honest. I
think he would like to be remembered as a man that gave everything
he had and when beaten, he got back up and tried again."[27]

◆◆◆

I remember my encounter with Coach McCracken. I was in junior
high school, and Branch had been retired a couple of years. He came to
our school to check on one of his student teachers. When he walked into
our gym, time seemed to just stop. I looked at our student teacher and
said, "That's Coach McCracken!" and he said, "Yes, that's the Sheriff."
(I thought, *No kidding—I know more about him than you.* Remember,
I was in junior high, but of course, I didn't say this. My parents had
taught me better than that.) I walked up the gym steps to the office and
introduced myself to Coach McCracken, holding out my right hand to
shake his while holding my left hand behind my back—it was shaking
way too much. Branch could not have been kinder to me as I thanked
him for all the years and everything he had done for IU. I knew right
then that my opinion of the man was correct:

He truly was a great man.

# Chapter 22

## MCCRACKEN'S HONORS AND RECORDS

*Branch receives Leather Medal Award,*
*April 30, 1940, from Sigma Delta Chi.*

1928 Honorable Mention Big Ten Football

1929 All-Conference Big Ten Football

All Big Ten Basketball 1928–1930

Helm Foundation Basketball All-American 1930

Finished career at Indiana as the Big Ten's All-Time Leading Scorer in Basketball

Small College Coach of the Year 1931 (Ball State)

Small College Coach of the Year 1938 (Ball State)

National Coach of the Year 1940 (Indiana)

National Coach of the Year 1953 (Indiana)

Helms Hall Coaches Hall of Fame 1958

Naismith Memorial Basketball Hall of Fame 1960

Indiana Basketball Hall of Fame 1963

Floor of Assembly Hall named after Branch McCracken, December 18, 1971

Charter member of Monroe County Hall of Fame 1976

Charter member of Indiana University Hall of Fame 1982

National Collegiate Basketball Hall of Fame 2006

Branch McCracken and John Wooden would be the only two consensus All-Americans to coach an NCAA Championship team in basketball

Branch McCracken remains the youngest coach to win an NCAA basketball championship by more than 3 years. He was 31 years, 9 months and 21 days old when the 1940 Indiana Hoosiers beat Kansas.

## Coaching Career Record

| Year | School | Wins | Losses |
|------|--------|------|--------|
| 1930–1931 | Ball State | 9 | 5 |
| 1931–1932 | Ball State | 9 | 7 |
| 1932–1933 | Ball State | 7 | 9 |
| 1933–1934 | Ball State | 9 | 10 |
| 1934–1935 | Ball State | 9 | 9 |
| 1935–1936 | Ball State | 13 | 7 |
| 1936–1937 | Ball State | 13 | 6 |
| 1937–1938 | Ball State | 17 | 4 |

| Year | School | Wins | Losses | Conference | Standings |
|------|--------|------|--------|-----------|-----------|
| 1938–1939 | Indiana | 17 | 3 | 9–3 | 2nd |
| 1939–1940 | Indiana | 20 | 3 | 9–3 | 2nd NCAA Champs |
| 1940–1941 | Indiana | 17 | 3 | 10–2 | 2nd |
| 1941–1942 | Indiana | 15 | 6 | 10–5 | T-2nd |
| 1942–1943 | Indiana | 18 | 2 | 11–2 | 2nd |
| War Years | | | | | |
| 1946–1947 | Indiana | 12 | 8 | 8–4 | T–2nd |
| 1947–1948 | Indiana | 8 | 12 | 3–9 | T–8th |
| 1948–1949 | Indiana | 14 | 8 | 6–6 | T–4th |
| 1949–1950 | Indiana | 17 | 5 | 7–5 | T–3rd |
| 1950–1951 | Indiana | 19 | 3 | 12–2 | 2nd |
| 1951–1952 | Indiana | 16 | 6 | 9–5 | 4th |

| | | | | | |
|---|---|---|---|---|---|
| 1952–1953 | Indiana | 23 | 3 | 17–1 | 1$^{st}$ NCAA Champs |
| 1953–1954 | Indiana | 20 | 4 | 12–2 | 1$^{st}$ |
| 1954–1955 | Indiana | 8 | 14 | 5–9 | T–6$^{th}$ |
| 1955–1956 | Indiana | 13 | 9 | 6–8 | T–6$^{th}$ |
| 1956–1957 | Indiana | 14 | 8 | 10–4 | T–1$^{st}$ |
| 1957–1958 | Indiana | 13 | 11 | 10–4 | 1$^{st}$ |
| 1958–1959 | Indiana | 11 | 11 | 7–7 | T–5$^{th}$ |
| 1959–1960 | Indiana | 20 | 4 | 11–3 | 2$^{nd}$ |
| 1960–1961 | Indiana | 15 | 9 | 8–6 | T–4$^{th}$ |
| 1961–1962 | Indiana | 14 | 9 | 7–7 | T–4$^{th}$ |
| 1962–1963 | Indiana | 13 | 11 | 9–5 | 3$^{rd}$ |
| 1963–1964 | Indiana | 9 | 15 | 5–9 | 8$^{th}$ |
| 1964–1965 | Indiana | 19 | 5 | 9–5 | 4$^{th}$ |
| 24 Years | Indiana | 364–174 | 677% | 216–113 | 657% |
| Overall | Indiana and Ball State | 450–231 | 661% | | |

*Branch in his last year as coach at Indiana, 1965 (Murphy Collection)*

# Notes

## Chapter 1

1. Jay T. Smith, producer, "Coach for Life" (Bloomington, IN: WTIU, 1989).

## Chapter 2

1. Jason Hiner, *Mac's Boys: Branch McCracken and the Legendary 1953 Hurryin' Hoosiers* (Bloomington, IN: Indiana University Press, 2006).

2. Jay T. Smith, producer, "Coach for Life" (Bloomington IN: WTIU, 1989).

3. *Arbutus*, Indiana University Yearbook, 1928.

4. Ibid.

5. Jay T. Smith, producer, "Coach for Life" (Bloomington IN: WTIU, 1989).

6. Ray Marquette, *Indiana University Basketball* (New York: Alpine Books, 1975).

7. Jay T. Smith, producer, "Coach for Life" (Bloomington IN: WTIU, 1989).

8. Ray Marquette, *Indiana University Basketball* (New York: Alpine Books, 1975).

## Chapter 3

1. Branch McCracken, *Indiana Basketball* (Englewood Cliffs, NJ: Prentice Hall, 1955).

## Chapter 4

1. Jay T. Smith, producer, "Coach for Life" (Bloomington, IN: WTIU, 1989).
2. Ibid.
3. Ray Marquette, *Indiana University Basketball* (New York: Alpine Books, 1975).
4. Jay T. Smith, producer, "Coach for Life" (Bloomington, IN: WTIU,1989).
5. *Orient*, Ball State University Yearbook, 1930.
6. Warren Vander Hill and Anthony O. Edmonds, *Ball State Men's Basketball 1918–2003* (Mount Pleasant, SC: Arcadia Publishing, 2003).
7. *Orient*, Ball State Yearbook, 1938.
8. *Orient*, Ball State Yearbook, 1938.

## Chapter 5

1. Ray Marquette, *Indiana University Basketball* (New York: Alpine Books, 1975).
2. Ibid.
3. Jay T. Smith, producer, "Coach for Life" (Bloomington, IN: WTIU,1989).

## Chapter 6

1. Pete DiPrimio and Rick Notter, *Hoosier Handbook: Stories, Stats, and Stuff About IU Basketball* (Wichita,KS: Midwest Sports Publications, 1995).

2. Ray Marquette, *Indiana University Basketball* (New York: Alpine Books, 1975).

3. Pete DiPrimio and Rick Notter, *Hoosier Handbook: Stories, Stats, and Stuff About IU Basketball* (Wichita, KS: Midwest Sports Publications, 1995).

4. Ray Marquette, *Indiana University Basketball* (New York: Alpine Books, 1975).

5. Pete DiPrimio and Rick Notter, *Hoosier Handbook: Stories, Stats, and Stuff About IU Basketball* (Wichita, KS: Midwest Sports Publications, 1995).

6. Jason Hiner, *Indiana University Basketball Encyclopedia* (Champaign, IL: Sports Publishing LLC, 2005).

7. Bloomington Dailey Telephone, March 1.

## Chapter 7

1. Pete DiPrimio and Rick Notter, *Hoosier Handbook: Stories, Stats, and Stuff About IU Basketball* (Wichita, KS: Midwest Sports Publications, 1995).

2. Ibid.

3. Jason Hiner, *Indiana University Basketball Encyclopedia* (Champaign, IL: Sports Publishing LLC, 2005).

4. Ray Marquette, *Indiana University Basketball* (New York: Alpine Books, 1975).

5. Indianapolis Times.

6. Pete DiPrimio and Rick Notter, *Hoosier Handbook: Stories, Stats, and Stuff About IU Basketball* (Wichita, KS: Midwest Sports Publications, 1995).

7. Ibid.

## Chapter 8

1. Jay T. Smith, producer, "Coach for Life" (Bloomington, IN: WTIU, 1989).
2. Ibid.
3. Ray Marquette, *Indiana University Basketball* (New York: Alpine Books, 1975).

## Chapter 9

1. Tom Graham and Rachel Graham Cody, *Getting Open: The Unknown Story of Bill Garrett and the Integration of College Basketball* (New York: Atria Books, 2006).
2. Ibid.
3. Ibid.
4. Jay T. Smith, producer, "Coach for Life" (Bloomington, IN: WTIU, 1989).
5. Tom Graham and Rachel Graham Cody, *Getting Open: The Unknown Story of Bill Garrett and the Integration of College Basketball* (New York: Atria Books, 2006).
6. Jay T. Smith, producer, "Coach for Life" (Bloomington, IN: WTIU, 1989).
7. Ibid.
8. Ray Marquette, *Indiana University Basketball* (New York: Alpine Books, 1975).
9. Ibid.
10. Jason Hiner, *Indiana University Basketball Encyclopedia* (Champaign, IL: Sports Publishing LLC, 2005).
11. Ibid.
12. Tom Graham and Rachel Graham Cody, *Getting Open: The Unknown Story of Bill Garrett and the Integration of College Basketball* (New York: Atria Books, 2006).
13. Ibid.

# Chapter 10

1. Jay T. Smith, producer, "Coach for Life" (Bloomington, IN: WTIU, 1989).

# Chapter 11

1. Brad Lennon, personal communication with author, 2013.

# Chapter 12

1. Pete DiPrimio and Rick Notter, *Hoosier Handbook: Stories, Stats, and Stuff About IU Basketball* (Wichita, KS: Midwest Sports Publications, 1995).

# Chapter 13

1. Jason Hiner, *Indiana University Basketball Encyclopedia* (Champaign, IL: Sports Publishing LLC, 2005).
2. Ibid.
3. Pete DiPrimio and Rick Notter, *Hoosier Handbook: Stories, Stats, and Stuff About IU Basketball* (Wichita, KS: Midwest Sports Publications, 1995).
4. Ibid.

# Chapter 14

(Does not apply)

# Chapter 15

1. Jason Hiner, *Indiana University Basketball Encyclopedia* (Champaign, IL: Sports Publishing LLC, 2005).
2. Jay T. Smith, producer, "Coach for Life" (Bloomington, IN: WTIU, 1989)

3. Indiana Daily Student, 1957.

4. Tom Miller, Indiana University Basketball Guide, 1957–58.

## Chapter 16

1. *Arbutus*, Indiana University Yearbook, 1958.

2. Ray Pavey, personal communication with author, 2013.

3. Ibid.

## Chapter 17

1. Jason Hiner, *Indiana University Basketball Encyclopedia* (Champaign, IL: Sports Publishing LLC, 2005).

2. Pete DiPrimio and Rick Notter, *Hoosier Handbook: Stories, Stats, and Stuff About IU Basketball* (Wichita, KS: Midwest Sports Publications, 1995).

## Chapter 18

1. Jay T. Smith, producer, "Coach for Life" (Bloomington, IU: WTIU, 1989).

2. Ibid.

3. Ray Pavey, personal communication with author, 2013.

4. Tom Bolyard, personal communication with author, 2013.

5. Ray Pavey, personal communication with author, 2013.

6. Ibid.

7. Jimmy Angelopolous, "Indiana's Big Bell," *Sport*, January, 1961.

8. Ray Pavey, personal communication with author, 2013.

9. Ibid.

10. Ibid.

11. Jason Hiner, *Indiana University Basketball Encyclopedia* (Champaign, IL: Sports Publishing LLC, 2005).

12. Pete DiPrimio and Rick Notter, *Hoosier Handbook: Stories, Stats, and Stuff About IU Basketball* (Wichita, KS: Midwest Sports Publications, 1995).

13. Dick Sparks, personal communication with author, 2013.

14. Ray Pavey, personal communication with author, 2013.

15. Jay T. Smith, producer, "Coach for Life" (Bloomington, IN: WTIU, 1989).

16. Tom Bolyard, personal communication with author, 2013.

17. Jay T. Smith, producer, "Coach for Life" (Bloomington, IN: WTIU, 1989).

18. Tom Bolyard, personal communication with author, 2013.

19. Ray Pavey, personal communication with author, 2013.

20. Ibid.

21. Ibid.

22. Tom Bolyard, personal communication with author, 2013.

## Chapter 18

1. Jay T. Smith, producer, "Coach for Life" (Bloomington, IN: WTIU, 1989).

2. Ibid.

3. Jay T. Smith, producer, "Coach for Life" (Bloomington, IN: WTIU, 1989).

## Chapter 19

1. Tom Miller, Indiana University Basketball Guide, 1963–64.

2. Larry Cooper, personal communication with author, 2013.

3. Ibid.

4. Pete DiPrimio and Rick Notter, *Hoosier Handbook: Stories, Stats, and Stuff About IU Basketball* (Wichita, KS: Midwest Sports Publications, 1995).

5.  Tom Miller, Indiana University Basketball Guide 1964–65.

6.  Larry Cooper, personal communication with author, 2013.

7.  Dave McCracken, personal communication with author, 2013.

8.  Kerry D. Marshall, *Two of a Kind: The Tom and Dick Van Arsdale Story* (Indianapolis, IN: Scott Publications, 1992).

9.  Jay T. Smith, producer, "Coach for Life" (Bloomington, IN: WTIU, 1989).

## Chapter 20

1.  Jay T. Smith, producer, "Coach for Life" (Bloomington, IN: WTIU, 1989).

2.  Pete DiPrimio and Rick Notter, *Hoosier Handbook: Stories, Stats, and Stuff About IU Basketball* (Wichita, KS: Midwest Sports Publications, 1995).

3.  Ibid.

4.  Jay T. Smith, producer, "Coach for Life" (Bloomington, IN: WTIU, 1989).

5.  Tom Bolyard, personal communication with author, 2013.

6.  Jade Butcher, personal communication with author, 2013.

7.  Jay T. Smith, producer, "Coach for Life" (Bloomington, IN: WTIU, 1989).

8.  Indiana Basketball Program, December 18, 1971.

## Chapter 21

1.  Pete DiPrimio and Rick Notter, *Hoosier Handbook: Stories, Stats, and Stuff About IU Basketball* (Wichita, KS: Midwest Sports Publications, 1995).

2.  Lynn Houser, Herald Times, January 9, 2007.

3. Pete DiPrimio and Rick Notter, *Hoosier Handbook: Stories, Stats, and Stuff About IU Basketball* (Wichita, KS: Midwest Sports Publications, 1995).

4. Ibid.

5. Ibid.

6. Dave Erdman, producer, "And This was Branch" (Bloomington, IN: WTIU, 1971).

7–17. Ibid.

18. Pete DiPrimio and Rick Notter, *Hoosier Handbook: Stories, Stats, and Stuff About IU Basketball* (Wichita, KS: Midwest Sports Publications, 1995).

19. Jay T. Smith, producer, "Coach for Life" (Bloomington, IN: WTIU, 1989).

20. Ibid.

21. Ibid.

22. Ibid.

23. Ibid.

24. Pete DiPrimio and Rick Notter, *Hoosier Handbook: Stories, Stats, and Stuff About IU Basketball* (Wichita, KS: Midwest Sports Publications, 1995).

25. Jay T. Smith, producer, "Coach for Life" (Bloomington, IN: WTIU, 1989).

26. Tom Miller, Indiana University Basketball Guide, 1965–66.

27. Jay T. Smith, producer, "Coach for Life" (Bloomington, IN: WTIU, 1989).

CPSIA information can be obtained at www.ICGtesting.com
Printed in the USA
LVOW12*2047190914

405007LV00002B/55/P